DAILY CANDY

D1443281

DAILY
CANDY
A to Z

illustrations by
Sujean Rim

DAILY CANDY
A to Z

AN INSIDER'S GUIDE TO THE SWEET LIFE

by the editors of
DailyCandy

Collins

First
published
in 2006 by Collins,
an imprint of Harper Collins
Publishers Ltd. 77-85 Fulham Palace
Road, London W6 8JB. The Collins
website address is *www.collins.co.uk*
The Daily Candy website address
is *www.dailycandy.com* Collins is a
registered trademark of Harp-
erCollins Publishers Ltd.

09 08 07 06
9 8 7 6 5 4 3 2 1
ISBN-10 0 00
724254 9 ISBN-13
978 0 00 724254 2

Text © Daily
Candy, 2006 Illus-
trations © Sujean Rim,
2006 Colour reproduction
by Colourscan, Singapore
Printed and bound by
Printing Express,
Hong Kong

designed by
Number Seventeen

to our readers—
WITHOUT YOU,
WE'RE NOTHING

CONTENTS

A
APPEARANCE
PAGE 1

B
BRAIN CANDY
PAGE 11

C
CHARM
PAGE 23

D
DO-GOODING
PAGE 31

E
EDIBLES
PAGE 37

F
FUNDAMENTALS
PAGE 45

G
GIRLS & GUYS
PAGE 51

H
HOME
PAGE 57

I
INTIMACY
PAGE 65

J
JET-SETTING
PAGE 79

K
KIN
PAGE 89

L
LUXURY
PAGE 99

M
MONEY
PAGE 107

N

NEVER
PAGE 113

O

OFFSPRING
PAGE 119

P

PARTY
PAGE 129

Q

QUANDARIES
PAGE 137

R

RITUAL
PAGE 145

S

SCORE
PAGE 157

T

TAKING A MOMENT
PAGE 165

U

UPHEAVAL
PAGE 171

V

VICE
PAGE 179

W

WORK
PAGE 189

X

X
PAGE 197

Y

YIKES
PAGE 205

Z

ZEITGEIST
PAGE 211

WHAT?
CAN IT BE?

DailyCandy, those traffickers in the transient, those peerless pur-
veyors of online editorial pith—writing a book? Is it possible? Is
it . . . wise?

Funny you should ask. We posed the same question. Pondered the
propriety of departing from our genre of the witty daily e-mail.
Wondered if we could possibly have enough to say. Feared no one
would care.

To which our editors answered: Um, we're not paying you to
ask questions.

So we set out to write. And the more we thought about it, the more
we realized: Of *course* we have enough to say. We have buttloads to
say. We never shut *up*. And while this probably shouldn't qualify
someone to write a book, the bestseller lists beg to differ. And hey,
they make the rules, not us.

Emboldened by the good news, we pressed on. And on. And on.
(Books, as it turns out, are long.) And now, we proudly present to
you the fruit of our labors: *DailyCandy A to Z: An Insider's Guide to
the Sweet Life.*

If you're familiar with DailyCandy.com, you know that despite our
reputation for brevity, we are tireless know-it-alls. We live to tell
our readers about the things we're jazzed about, whether it's a new

restaurant, an undiscovered jewelry designer, or a wacky beauty secret. Launched over six years ago in New York City, DailyCandy has grown from a one-woman operation into a band of plucky fun-seekers across the globe, with daily versions in New York, London, Los Angeles, Chicago, San Francisco, Boston, Dallas, Washington, D.C., and Everywhere (our national version), as well as weekly editions dedicated to Travel, Kids, and Deals. At this point, DailyCandy isn't just an e-mail in your in-box; it's a state of mind, a view of the world that strives every day to find that sweet spot where coolness, self-deprecating humor, information, and entertainment overlap.

DailyCandy A to Z is our chance to shed the confines of our signature two-hundred-word, read-it-over-your-morning-coffee daily e-mail and talk at greater length about, well, lots of stuff. Inside you'll find musings on everything from first-date sex to mothers and their martyr-speak to, of course, sample-sale etiquette. In some ways, it's not so different from what you'll find on the DailyCandy site. For newcomers, this book will serve as an introduction; for fans it will deepen and generally enrich your experience of the DailyCandy universe.

And while it may come as a surprise to some, this book is in fact the logical culmination of everything we've been working on for the past six years. Our stock in trade may be the ephemera of commerce and culture, but the route it's taken us on has been long and rewarding. Plus, as we mentioned, we do like to carry on. To those of you who know DailyCandy well, the writing was on the wall (or, rather, the computer screen) all along.

is for
APPEARANCE

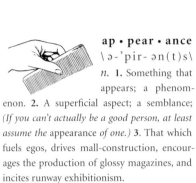

ap • pear • ance
\ə-'pir-ən(t)s\
n. **1.** Something that appears; a phenom-enon. **2.** A superficial aspect; a semblance; *(If you can't actually be a good person, at least assume the* appearance *of one.)* **3.** That which fuels egos, drives mall-construction, encour-ages the production of glossy magazines, and incites runway exhibitionism.

CLOSE YOUR EYES AND DARE TO IMAGINE A PERFECT WORLD

in which appearance doesn't matter. You roll out of bed, skip your shower, ignore the atrocious zit that has installed itself on your chin overnight, embrace the greasy bedhead look, and greet the world wearing whatever you slept in.

Then again, that's precisely the routine Morris, the sweaty guy in the cubicle next to yours, followed today, as well. Ditto the people in your yoga class, your boss, and your significant other.

Now open your eyes and give thanks for the petty, superficial laws governing human interaction—not only because they prevent our workplaces and public spaces from becoming festering petri dishes, but because they provide us with yet another stage upon which to express ourselves, compete, communicate, and bond.

The next few pages are about looking good. But more than that, they're about finding the right way to look like *you*—to have fun with what you've been given, and find your place in the ever-shifting realms of style and beauty.

What you put on, do with, or don't do with your body is your business.
But as you're well aware, people look and judge. Is this fair? No. Can it be changed?
No. What to do 'bout that? Something, fer sure. Have fun with it.

FAT DAYS
Blame It on the Dryer

If the world were a kinder place, employers would grant allotted "fat days" during which one could lie on the couch and watch daytime television while successfully avoiding reflective surfaces. Alas. Life is cruel.

In truth, the pint of Ben & Jerry's you mauled last night didn't move you up a dress size. But it sure feels that way. A few tips on getting through the day:

1. **PASS THE BUCK.** It's not the hot wings you just devoured that are making you feel large; it's those crazy jeans made from "Italian denim"! That stuff shrinks up in the dryer like a sun-dried tomato in the Mediterranean sun.

2. **SURE, GO SHOPPING**—but only at well-lit-boutiques. Dressing-room mirrors in department stores are awful indicators of the truth. Don't think for one second that the washed-out person with superlong arms, extra-wide hips, and more ripples than a potato chip is actually you. It's that God-awful fluorescent lighting, which demolishes your skin tone, turns your highlights an aggressive shade of puce, makes your cellulite look like a "before" commercial, and renders your blemishes worthy of an ad for Clearasil. Also remember: Would you really stand six inches from your mirror to inspect your outfit at home?

3. **TUMMY-HOLDING-IN PANTIES** work miracles. Just make sure no one actually sees them . . .

4. **REMEMBER THAT SIZING** is different for practically every label.

HELP ME, FONDA
GYM ATTIRE DOS AND DON'TS

Not to sound judgmental, but people who troll for dates at their local gym are pathetic. (That doesn't sound judgmental, does it?) The gym is neither a pickup parlor nor a couture catwalk.

Still, you never know who you may run into—ex-boyfriend, potential boyfriend, business associate—and there's certainly no reason to look more revolting than necessary while plodding away on that treadmill. Some pointers on proper workout wear:

DO	DON'T
• Invest in solid-color basics that you can mix and match.	• Wear dirty gym clothes. This officially makes you disgusting. One way to avoid being a skank is to take your gym clothes with you into the shower and let them hang to dry for tomorrow.
• Bust out the fun shirts. You have a drawer full of tees you wouldn't dare wear to work. In other words, it's time to break out the "Rabbi's Daughter" number or that "My grandma went to Tucson and all I got was this lousy T-shirt" tee.	• Turn, even in the direst bottom-of-the-drawer moment, to that old thong-leotard-over-spandex get-up. That should be reserved for costume parties.
• White socks. No exceptions. Pom-poms are acceptable if you're feeling bold.	• Wear baggy pants/shirts.
• Combine two different strap-types. While not acceptable in daily life, the racer-back/tank combo mysteriously looks pretty rockin' with gym wear.	• Get overly skimpy. You're not here to turn tricks, and you don't want your boob flying out during a downward dog or enthusiastic aerobics routine.
	• Two words: bum bag.

FEELING CRAPPY, LOOKING SNAPPY

A Primer

7:24 A.M. *Wake up, yawn, stretch, hit snooze.*

7:34 A.M. *Wake up, yawn, stretch, hit snooze.*

7:44 A.M. *Wake up, yawn, stretch, stumble to bathroom.*

7:45 A.M. *Suppress screams of horror upon catching sight of self in bathroom mirror.*

7:46 A.M. *Return to bed. Attempt to forget past twelve minutes.*

We all have days when we feel like someone's been whacking us all night long with the ugly stick covered with ashes. When that one pinhead-size zit looks like an angry Vesuvius. When we want to unzip our skin and crawl out of our body.

Three words: Get over it. In all likelihood, you look no different than you did yesterday—and the world just isn't going to notice. So chin up. And get started on making yourself feel and look better.

1. INVEST IN A GOOD CONCEALER AND FOUNDATION. The appearance of flawless skin leaves you looking rested and healthy. Finding the right shade is key, so take your time when searching for one that matches your complexion. (Nothing draws attention to flaws like dry, ghostly blotches of concealer.) Furthermore, knowing

how to apply the stuff can be tricky. Make sure you have the best tools: Applying concealer with a brush will give you the most control over the amount of coverage and blending.

2. HAVE AN EMERGENCY OUTFIT. You should always have one outfit that you know you feel confident and comfortable in. In choosing it, keep the following in mind: It's something you don't wear too often (hence, it should be available for emergencies). Basics paired with cool accessories work best. A few possible EOs: Black jeans and white tank with a killer pair of shoes. (Never underestimate the power of shoes. They detract from the rest of you.) Or, a strappy dress with a bit of wiggle room for those days you feel like a cow.

3. TAKE TIME TO CHILL OUT. If you're feeling awful and you find yourself freaking out, take a few minutes to drink a cup of tea and clear your mind.

4. A GOOD SONG can brighten your mood and your look any day.

5. LARGE SUNGLASSES COVER TIRED EYES. And they make you seem like a faux celebrity. Just don't wear them inside.

6. DON'T TRY TO HIDE UNDER LARGE SWEATERS, hats, or anything that resembles something you wear to bed. This only draws attention to your disposition.

7. HAVE A HAIRSTYLE TO FALL BACK ON. Similar to the emergency outfit, this is a quick and easy solution that requires little stress on your part. In other words, don't attempt the beehive style you thought looked so great in this month's *Vogue*. It could make things worse.

8. DON'T ACT LIKE YOU FEEL LIKE HELL. A smile is all you need to convince others that you're feeling great.

CANDY LIBS

So I woke up this morning and realized I looked like crap.

Immediate action was necessary. I started with my hair.

I decided to get_____inches taken off.
NUMBER

Only I wanted a little more definition, so I asked for some

layering around my_____. Next, I dyed my hair
FEATURE

a_____shade of_____with_____
ADJECTIVE   COLOR   DIFFERENT COLOR

highlights. Of course I needed a_____palette
ADJECTIVE

to complement my hair. I got some 100%_____
ADJECTIVE

foundation, pale_____blush, and a bunch of new-
COLOR

fangled eyeliners that you apply with a_____at
NOUN

_____. I also got some_____makeup
NAME OF STORE   ADJECTIVE

brushes. (Oh, and a jumbo Kit Kat—I couldn't resist.)

Then I went shopping. I got a_____that shows off my
ARTICLE OF CLOTHING

legs, and a pair of_____that make me look really
KIND OF SHOES

_____. I decided to go for the whole_____trend
ADJECTIVE   DECADE

that's so big right now, so I got a vintage_____and
ACCESSORY

_____ _____. When I was done, I couldn't
TYPE OF FABRIC   GARMENT

believe it. I looked_____, just like_____.
ADJECTIVE   CELEBRITY

BEYOND APPEARANCES: FROM B TO Z

We started this chapter with a plea for the importance of appearance, and we have no regrets. However, this is only the beginning. That "Appearance" is the first chapter of *DailyCandy A to Z* is somewhat apropos; while we stress the value of caring for and enjoying your looks, we also want you to keep in mind the vast world that lies beyond in the pages to come.

So indulge us as we totally go back on what we said earlier and remind you that appearances are just that—surface qualities that may please and delight, but are far from the whole story. Always enjoy the pleasure appearances can bring; never ever judge someone by them.

is for
BRAIN CANDY

brain can • dy \'brān' 'kan-dē\ *n.*
1. Something that amuses, pleases, or diverts. *(I'm bored! I need some brain candy.)* **2.** The must-see movie, the must-read book, the must-hear CD. **3.** The way we spend our time when not working, eating, sleeping, or smooching.

INSIDE THAT HEAD OF YOURS

dwells a mysterious glob of God-knows-what, which we call your brain. This hard-working mass of squiggles* is home to just about everything you think of as your "self": your intellect, your feelings, your identity, your ability to move, see, taste, hear, understand, and resent other people for being prettier or better dressed.

This chapter is all about doing nice things for your brain. Don't worry, there are no boring summer-reading lists or self-help books here: We at DailyCandy believe that "culture" should be synonymous with "fun" (except when used in conjunction with "throat"). And while we'll touch on a number of subjects, this is by no means intended as an exhaustive guide to all things intellectually edifying. We're here to entertain, not to lull you into a torpid state of suicidal ennui. If that's what you're looking for, we suggest graduate school.

*In case our use of the term "mass of squiggles" to refer to your brain hasn't tipped you off, we're not medical professionals or scientists. Consult your doctor before taking anything, especially if you're pregnant, nursing, ill, or on other medications.

Whether it's becoming completely engrossed by the riveting text on the back of a box of Rice Krispies or starting a book club, nothing rivals the printed page for educational value, mind-expansion, and sheer escapism.

CLUBBING
IOI

Starting Your Own Book Club

Think book clubs are only for fat, earnest ladies? Nonsense! Oprah lost all that weight, and she's still totally rocking hers. Plus, with a little outside-the-Harry-Potter-box-set thinking, you can tailor your club to meet your needs and pique your interests. So round up the posse, pop those mini pizza bagels into the oven, break out the pinot grigio, and consider these alternatives.

1. A READ-TO-ME CLUB. Members take turns reading chapters aloud to the group. Sure, it takes longer to get through each tome, but it ensures that a) everyone's on the same page (literally), and b) people are actually reading. (You want to weed out ingrates, illiterates, and lazy slackers right off the bat.) Poetry is also a good option; or plays, where each member reads a different role.

GOOD FOR: MOTIVATED TYPES, THE BLIND

BAD FOR: STUTTERERS, THE SHY, THE DEAF

2. BOOKS-AND-THEIR-ADAPTATIONS READING/VIEWING CLUB. Though '70s TV shows seem to be providing an endless

stream of material for unoriginal moviemakers looking to cash in on someone else's ideas, there are still plenty of unoriginal moviemakers trying to cash in on the ideas of writers. From works by Michael Crichton to Jane Austen, lots of novels get adapted into films each year. Read the book, then attend a showing as a group. Then spend the rest of the evening talking about how much better the book was.

GOOD FOR: MULTIMEDIA ENTHUSIASTS

BAD FOR: PARTY POOPERS

3. A TWO-PERSON BOOK CLUB. A great way for couples to find yet another thing to argue about. Alternate choosing the books and discuss to whatever extent you wish—one couple we know restricts their comments to "What page are *you* on?"

GOOD FOR: SHY COUPLES

BAD FOR: LONERS

4. A MAGAZINE CLUB. Don't forget the most popular print medium around. Meet to discuss the latest *New Yorker* (smarty-pants), or choose a different publication every week. Fashion buffs can use the time to share thoughts on the latest collections in *Vogue*, *Bazaar*, and *Lucky*; music lovers can rate the scribblings of their favorite reviewers. It's a great way to keep up with current news in your preferred area, and the perfect opportunity to seek out like-minded readers.

GOOD FOR: MOST TYPES

BAD FOR: HOPELESS SNOBS

5. A BOOKS-ON-TAPE CLUB. This can be a good way in to more difficult writers, like William Faulkner or James Joyce. Just about anything you'd want to read has been recorded by some aging Shakespearean actor looking to make a few bucks.

GOOD FOR: PEOPLE WITH LONG COMMUTES

BAD FOR: BAD DRIVERS

GOTTA GET HIGH TO GET LOW

Match the original work to the later adaptation

MOVIE	BOOK/PLAY
A. *Rent*	**1.** *Romeo and Juliet*
B. *My Own Private Idaho*	**2.** *Persuasion*
C. *West Side Story*	**3.** *Henry IV, parts 1 & 2*
D. *Bridget Jones: The Edge of Reason*	**4.** *La Bohème*
E. *Clueless*	**5.** *The Wizard of Oz*
F. *A Thousand Acres*	**6.** *King Lear*
G. *Wicked*	**7.** *Emma*

ANSWERS: 1C; 2D; 3B; 4A; 5G; 6F; 7E

CROSS PURPOSES
Mastering the Puzzle

Think only smart people are good at crosswords? Wrong. Those smug bastards just happen to know something you don't—a bunch of words, most of which start with vowels, none of which you'd ever want to use in real life, and which for some reason tend to show up in these puzzles again and again. Below, a cheat sheet.

ADAR
A Hebrew month

AERIE
A nest
(sometimes "aery")

ALIT
Past tense of "alight,"
to settle on
(as a bird on a branch)

APED
Past tense of
"to ape," or to imitate
(Also: aper)

AVER
To state or affirm

EERY
Alternate spelling
of "eerie"

EIRE
Ireland

ELUL
Another Hebrew month

ERMA
First name of
Erma Bombeck,
American humorist

GMAN
(really, G-man)
an IRS agent

IMAM
Muslim prayer leader

IRAE
Latin for "wrath";
the answer to the clue
Dies____.

ISAK
First name of Danish writer
Isak Dinesen

OBI
A belt for a kimono

OBOE
A wind instrument

ODIN
Norse god and creator

OLEG
First name of Oleg Cassini,
fashion designer

OLEO
Margarine

OMOO
Novel by Herman Melville

OREL
First name of
Orel Hershiser,
baseball pitcher

OVOID
Egg-shaped

OVUM,OVA
Egg, eggs

*Not to be a downer, but the human mind has come up with
some pretty horrific crap. H-bombs, fascism, infomercials, huevos Spamcheros…
the list goes on. But we make up for it in one fell swoop. With music.*

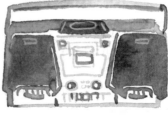

MIXED MESSAGES

Building the Soundtrack of Your Life

People used to buy these things called "albums." They were big and
flat and had a bunch of songs on one side and a bunch of songs on
the other, and usually you would listen to a whole album all the way
through. No, really.

These days, attempting to expose your friends to a whole hour of
music by a single artist would be tantamount to inviting them to
dinner and serving them a seven-course meal. Hence, it's important in these iTunes-driven times to familiarize yourself with the
concept of the "mix," once only the mysterious province of the DJ.

1. CHOOSE YOUR THEME. Whether as background for cocktails,
a cross-country drive, to exercise to, or a love letter, most mixes serve
a specific purpose. Decide the purpose of your mix—a CD that's
meant to convey the sentiment "Be My Valentine" will be very different from one that says "You Need to Bathe More Often."

2. VARY THE MIX. You may detect vast differences among the
various subgenres that comprise the neo-folk movement, but it all
sounds like the same warbly crap to the rest of us. Go ahead, put
some Devendra Banhart on there. But then shake things up with a
bit of AC/DC or Violent Femmes. Keep them guessing, and they'll be
on the edge of their seats.

3. **MAINTAIN A THROUGH-LINE.** The entire mix should function as one complete statement. Public Enemy and Elvis Costello? If you must. Public Enemy and Debussy? Might be a stretch.

4. **PAY ATTENTION TO THE ORDER.** Like a short story or a movie, listening to a mix is usually a linear experience—and as such it needs an overall trajectory, as well as an internal structure, complete with crescendos, transitions, reprieves, and interludes. If you need to get from Air Supply's "All Out of Love" to the Sex Pistols' "Pretty Vacant" in the next three songs, think about how you're going to get there.

HOOKED ON CLASSICS:

HOW MUCH DO YOU KNOW ABOUT CLASSICAL MUSIC?

1. A *fugue* is:

a) a type of wind instrument.

b) a compositional form.

c) a feud between two sections of an orchestra.

d) a nickname for a snooty conductor.

2. Romantic composer Brahms's first name was:

a) Ludwig.

b) Antonin.

c) Django.

d) Johannes.

3. A *string quartet* consists of a violin, a viola, a cello, and:

a) another violin.

b) another cello.

c) a piano.

d) a harp.

4. The Waldstein Sonata was written by:

a) Bach.

(b) Mozart.

(c) Beethoven.

(d) Waldstein.

5. Handel's *Messiah* is sung in which language?

a) German

b) Latin

c) English

d) Esperanto

ANSWERS:
1B; 2D; 3A; 4C; 5C

(SUPPLE)MENTAL HEALTH
HOW TO INCREASE YOUR BRAIN POWER LEGALLY

These days you don't have to settle for what you were born with—whether it's your income bracket, your boobs, or your IQ. With all the supplements out there, there's really no excuse for feeblemindedness.

SUPPLEMENT	WHAT IT IS	WHAT IT DOES	WHERE TO GET IT
GINKGO BILOBA	a 200-million-year-old tree	improves memory and concentration; combats depression; treats dizziness, tinnitus, and headaches	in a bottle, off the tree
VITAMIN B6	vitamin	aids in synthesis of neurotransmitters, improving mood and mental function	chicken, fish, pork, liver, kidney, whole grains, nuts, legumes, supplements
VITAMIN B12	vitamin	improves memory, concentration, and energy levels	liver, kidney, yogurt, dairy products, fish, clams, oysters, nonfat dry milk, salmon, sardines, supplements
TAURINE	amino acid	improves alertness and concentration, particularly in combination with caffeine	Red Bull, cat food, red wine, supplements
ST. JOHN'S WORT	flower found in the northwest United States	combats depression; reduces stress	supplements, teas, snack chips

WHEW. Talk about a mental workout. Being smart isn't all *Jeopardy!* championships and Nobel Prizes, you know—it takes work. But it's worth it, and not just because of all the compliments you get on being brainy *and* hot. The more intellectual curiosity you have, the more you'll get out of life.

So go on and dare to take that online Mensa quiz again. You may just find that you've climbed a few notches on the smart chart. And if not, never fear.

This is only chapter two.

You've still got a lot to learn.

is for
CHARM

charm \'chärm\ *n.* **1.** The power or quality of pleasing or enchanting. *(My friend Susie can* charm *her way into a business class upgrade like nobody's business.)* **2.** A certain flair cultivated and used as a means to get what we want, as in lovers, money, or lovers with money. **3.** A trinket. **4.** That intangible *je ne sais quoi* that draws us to someone. *(The rest of us were immune to Martin's alleged* charms, *but Josie was smitten.)*

ANY DEFINITION OF CHARM

is a tease. Because by its nature, charm is indefinable. Equal parts grace, warmth, style, and flair, it's a spell cast over unsuspecting (and suspecting), blissfully willing recipients. A true charmer can lull babies to sleep, make uptight librarians blush, and pretty much get his or her way in any situation.

Some are born with it. Others cultivate it (see: French and Italian men). And incidentally, there's a fine line between charm and smarm (see: French and Italian men). Here are some basics.

How can you become more charming? It's easier than you think.

CHARM
✿IN ACTION
The Seven and a Half Commandments

1. **ASK QUESTIONS.** It's amazing how interesting you become as soon as you ask a good question. Most people love talking about themselves. And they love it even more when you seem genuinely interested in what they say. Make eye contact, and act like the person you are talking to is the only one in the room. Crack jokes, tease, and be sure to let on little about yourself.

2. **BE PREPARED.** Charming people always have something to talk about in every situation, so know your material. The Middle East, the films of Michel Gondry, Yoda, the Rolling Stones, your favorite cuts of beef—anything will do. Do not, however, prepare and rehearse actual statements or jokes unless you want to sound canned and rehearsed. Oh, and read the paper, for goodness' sake.

3. **CARRY A CONVERSATION PIECE.** An interesting piece of jewelry, a gag gift, a scar, or even a funny-looking friend will do. People will be apt to inquire about it. When they do, have an anecdote at the ready ("Oh, these gloves? It all started when this baron bailed me out of prison . . .").

4. **BE UNEXPECTED.** After introductions, skip the obligatory "So what do you do?" and talk about something fun instead. One charmer always leads with "What have you been up to tonight?" Find yourself facing someone with whom you have absolutely nothing in common? Even better: Consider it an opportunity to learn about something new—or at least an occasion to push your values and ideals onto somebody else.

5. GESTICULATE WILDLY. Okay, not wildly. But a little hand motion can go a long way. Try adding a subtle snap, hand clap, or touch of charades to your next conversation. Why not?

6. SMILE AND LISTEN. Can't think of anything to say? Follow the conversation with an interested look, nod when appropriate, smile warmly, and for Chrissakes, listen! People will leave talking about what a wonderful person you are, even if they're not sure why.

7. IT'S NOT A CONTEST. Never one-up, no matter how tempted you are to respond with "Funny, that reminds of the time I was in my hot tub in my chalet in Gstaad!" Let others enjoy the spotlight.

7.5. IF ALL ELSE FAILS . . . Drink heavily. Just kidding. Well, a little.

Charm or Smarm? A CHECKLIST

Dramatic, nonintimidating gestures	CHARM	
Showing off		SMARM
Buying someone a drink	CHARM	
Sending flowers	CHARM	
Calling your mother	CHARM	
Calling their mother		SMARM
Too much cologne		SMARM
Unfathomably tight jeans		SMARM
"So nice to meet you."	CHARM	
"Do you know who I am?"		SMARM
Presuming you're beautiful	CHARM	
Presuming they think you're beautiful		SMARM

THE DEVIL IN THE DETAILS
SUBTLETIES THAT MATTER

How subtle are your verbal skills? Match the quality to
the statement that most exemplifies it and find out.

1. Charisma
2. Witty repartee
3. Flirtatious banter
4. Making others feel important
5. Genuine interest in others
6. Warmth
7. Graciousness
8. Generosity

(a) "So tell me again—do you really
own *four* piranhas?"

(b) "No, really, let me take care
of the check."

(c) "Martin, this is Jill, the best
interior decorator in town."

d) "Ashton thinks the Gaza Strip
is a club in Hollywood."

(e) "I dare you to make a pass at me."

(f) "I'm so pleased your brother
overcame his learning disorder."

(g) "No, please. After you."

(h) "Everybody form a conga line!"

ANSWERS: 1H; 2D; 3E; 4C; 5A; 6F; 7G; 8B

AMULETS AND EVIL EYES
Charms Through the Ages

The word "charm" and its various meanings can be traced back to objects, words, or incantations imbued with magical powers. Let's take a quick stroll through history to see just how long we've been under charm's spell.

600–1400 A.D.

750 B.C.–500 A.D.

ROMAN EMPIRE
Charms worn under garments allow people to gain entry into secret, forbidden activities of worship and debauchery. Kind of like a VIP membership to the Harvard Club. With slightly less distasteful displays of excess.

MEDIEVAL TIMES
Trinkets are used by witches in conjunction with incantations to protect knights and wreak havoc on enemies. Charms worn on belts represent family origin, political standing, and profession. Ladies of the court wear the charms of their suitors. Varsity jackets follow a few hundred years later.

1400–1600

1830–1900

VICTORIAN AGE
Queen Victoria revives charms and turns them into a fashion statement. Small lockets, glass beads, and family crests hang from bracelets, necklaces, and belt loops. Because she's so badass, charms become the rage.

THE RENAISSANCE
Charms fall out of style among those of the upper classes, who are temporarily distracted by the discovery of spatial depth and visions of muscular (and scantily clad) bodies on church ceilings.

3,000 B.C.

NEOLITHIC ERA
Unusual stones or other items
from nature are thought
to have specific powers to ward
off enemies and possibly
diminish unsightly hair growth.
(Which means that the
prehistoric precursors to
charms were also the
earliest depilatories.)

2700–100 B.C.

ANCIENT EGYPT
Pharaohs, obsessed with
the afterlife, make
elaborate charm bracelets
as ID tags to ensure their
status level after they die.
(Tut (+3) for the
Champagne room, please.)

2006

1945

21ST CENTURY
Anything goes in
the accessories department. But
overdo it and
you'll look like a walking
treasure chest.

POST-WWII
Soldiers leaving Europe
and islands in the Pacific purchase
trinkets to bring home to
their sweethearts. Craftsmen fashion small
bits of metal into little
replicas of items common
to the locale. American businesses catch
on and turn this into a profitable industry.
Capitalism at its finest.

ABOVE ALL, REMEMBER: true charm comes from with-in.
The most alluring thing you can do is to find ways to be yourself and share
your already wonderful personality with those around you. How to do that?
Funny you should ask. Doing good for others is a swell way to start, and it's
the subject of our next chapter.

is for
DO-GOODING

do-good · ing
\'dü-gu-din\ *n.* **1.**
The act of charitable
contribution. **2.** The
occasion for much self-congratulatory
indulgence. *(After a long day of do-
gooding at the Junior League, Muffy
liked to treat herself to a scotch or two.)*

SOME SAY THE WORLD IS DIVIDED INTO TWO TYPES:

the good, who spread love and lend a helping hand; and the bad, who avoid charitable activities, drop-kick puppies, and spit on babies.

In reality, most of us fall somewhere in between. And those filled with good intentions but are perhaps lacking in motivation don't deserve fire and brimstone—just a mini-kick in the pants to get us going in the right direction.

So, given that you're the amazingly principled person we believe you to be, we're going to help you get that do-gooding motor started with a few quick pointers for clearing away the obstacles that have kept you from getting off your duff.

OVERWHELMED? Think globally, act— Oh, you know the rest. That old new-age adage is as true now as it always has been. World hunger, homelessness, illness . . . these things all exist somewhere in your vicinity.

NERVOUS? Start in your comfort zone. Have social anxiety? Skip the soup kitchen and try one-on-one tutoring or mentoring. Fear all humans? Volunteer with animals.

IN A RUT? Get out of your comfort zone. If you're bored with life, volunteering can present new challenges. If you work in finance, try an arts program with disadvantaged kids. Work as a teacher, maybe look for a nursing home.

TIMID? Bring a friend. Plenty of places will let you buddy up with a pal, so find someone with a common interest and explore options together.

REALLY, REALLY LAZY? Donate money. Nobody will complain about that.

*We joke about helping the little old lady across the street, but when
do we actually do it? Not often enough. Not all charity work has to be over-the-top.
There are little things you can do that will make anyone smile.*

RANDOM ACTS OF
KINDNESS
*Not Just Something
Annoying on a
Bumper Sticker*

Is it really about the little things? Yes. Especially when those things
make someone else's day brighter. And it doesn't take much. Here are
nine things that can make a big difference.

1
BRING COFFEE TO YOUR MAIL-, DOOR-, OR DELIVERY PERSON.

2
WHEN YOU GET GREAT SERVICE,
WRITE A LETTER TO THE PERSON'S SUPERVISOR

3
PUT CHANGE IN SOMEONE'S EXPIRED PARKING METER.

4
PAY THE TOLL FOR THE PERSON BEHIND YOU.

5
HOLD THE DOOR OPEN FOR SOMEONE.

6
OFFER TO CARRY ANOTHER PERSON'S GROCERIES.

7
LET THE GUY IN A HURRY CUT IN FRONT OF YOU.

8
TELL SOMEONE TO KEEP THE CHANGE. AND MEAN IT.

9
TAKE CARE OF YOUR FRIEND'S/SIGNIFICANT
OTHER'S LIBRARY BOOK FINES.

BAD COMPANY
THINGS THAT SEEM LIKE GOOD DEEDS BUT AREN'T

Some things only seem like a good idea.
Pause and think seriously before doing any of the following:

1. Forwarding good-luck chain e-mails.
Yes, you have a day job. And so do your friends.

2. Giving up your seat on the bus
to a woman you aren't *absolutely sure* is pregnant.

3. Using a "cheaper" calling service when you call collect.

4. Saving the last swig of
Diet Pepsi for your significant other.

5. Not telling people they have food stuck in their teeth.

6. Not telling someone their flies are undone.

GIFTING THROUGH THE RUBBISH

Giving: is it *really* better than receiving? Yes. At least we think so. And it's not always about handing over money. Your time is just as valuable. Which is why we are keeping this chapter short and sweet—so you'll put down this book and pick up a hammer, or some canned goods for a local food pantry. A little will always go a long way with people in need. As the immortal protagonist of *Clueless* so brilliantly paraphrased, "'Tis a far better thing doing stuff for others."

is for
EDIBLES

ed • i • bles \'e-də-bəlz\ *n.* **1.** Items fit to be eaten. *(Carrie, check out the* edibles *spread on the antipasto table.)* **2.** A legitimate justification to leave the office. *(If I don't get my hands on something* edible *ASAP I'm going to fall over.)* **3.** The object of much guilt and obsession. **4.** The means by which we thrive, and therefore a cause for celebration.

TECHNICALLY SPEAKING,

you could survive for the rest of your life without ever again taking a vacation, going to a party, doing a good deed, or buying a new pair of heels. (We didn't say it would be fun. We just said you *could*.) But you could never go through life without food. Not only would you never want to, but you simply wouldn't last very long. (You listening, crash dieters and compulsive fasters?)

Food is sustenance—the stuff of life and love. Meals are the medium by which we celebrate holidays, weddings, and romances; seal business deals; or simply read the newspaper and zone. Just try to think of an occasion that isn't improved by a platter of figs and cheese, a bowl of pappardelle, or a side of short ribs.

Frankly, we're amazed we made it all the way to "E" without some serious nibbling.

THE GOOD, THE BAD, AND THE STUPID
A Word About Diets

If you're alive and a woman, chances are you have been on, are on, or will at some point in your life go on a diet. This is a bad thing if you can't remember the last time you weren't on a diet. This is a fine thing if you realize that every so often you need to pay attention to the quality (and quantity) of what you're eating. It's totally unrealistic to hope to look like a lingerie model (most lingerie models don't even look like lingerie models without airbrushing), but it's hard to dispute that slim people are generally healthier. On a path littered with experimentations with countless fad (raw, bacon, liquid) diets, we picked up a few tips:

SURE-FIRE SIGNS YOUR DIET WILL FAIL

you're allowed to eat bacon

you're allowed to eat brie

you lose more than two pounds per week

you eat more processed food
(protein bars, soy crisps)
than real food (tomatoes, blueberries)

it involves the intake
of more than 2 pills a day

you can't eat carbs, ever

the plan has been endorsed
by a B-list celeb

you're not preparing any of your own food

SURE-FIRE SIGNS YOUR DIET WILL SUCCEED

you lose weight slowly and steadily

you eat everything in the right amounts

you don't dream about food all day long

you're eating balanced meals

you're also exercising

WHAT YOUR FRIDGE SAYS ABOUT YOU

CONTENTS

EMPTY THAI TAKEOUT CARTON (THREE DAYS OLD)

MINI-BOTTLES OF HEINZ KETCHUP AND BONNE MAMAN WILD BERRIES JAM

BOTTLES OF PERFUME AND MOISTURIZER

PARMALAT MILK

VEUVE CLICQUOT CHAMPAGNE

SEVEN 1.5-LITER BOTTLES OF EVIAN

WHO YOU ARE

A model (you're afraid to eat), a stewardess (you're never home),
an investment banker (you don't even know where the fridge is)

CONTENTS

FROZEN TV DINNERS	FROZEN PILLSBURY COOKIE DOUGH (HALF EATEN)
POP-TARTS	
MEUNSTER CHEESE	ENGLISH MUFFINS
COKE ONE	I CAN'T BELIEVE IT'S NOT BUTTER

WHO YOU ARE

Jane America (self-admitted addict of processed food
and partially hydrogenated corn syrup)

CONTENTS

OLIVE PASTE	FENNEL
ANCHOVIES	ORGANIC BASIL
MAILLE DIJON MUSTARD	DRY ITALIAN *SALAMINI*
TRUFFLE HONEY	TWO BOTTLES OF TOKAI
ONE HEAD OF TREVISO RADICCHIO	

WHO YOU ARE

A professor of Italian literature (and you wish you
were back home in Bologna), a food snob (and why are you keeping
your honey in the fridge, dingbat?)

Okay, who loves eating out? Whoa – it's unanimous. Not having to shop
or cook? No cleaning up? Let us count the ways. Of course,
there are certain things you really must know before making that reservation.
Starting, of course, with how to look like you belong.

NEXT TIME,
WE'RE STAYING HOME
More Annoying Restaurant Habits

CHARTED ON AN ANNOYING SCALE FROM ONE TO TEN

1: DO OTHER PEOPLE ACTUALLY LIKE THIS?

"Hi! I'm Darren, and I'll be your waiter this evening."

"Would you like fresh pepper with that?"
(Inevitably offered before you've tasted your food.)

3: IS IT JUST ME OR IS THIS ANNOYING?

"*Jus*" "Foam" "Reduction" "Hint of"

"How is everything?"
(Inevitably asked before you've tasted anything.)

5: IT'S NOT ME. THIS IS ANNOYING.

Referring to the chef as "chef."
As in, "Chef recommends the *sous vide* squab served
with a parsley and persimmon *jus*."

7: PERHAPS I SHOULD SPEAK WITH THE MANAGER?

Automatically tacking 20 percent service charge onto check.

10: NO TIP, JACKASS.

"We'll need a credit card to hold that
Monday night reservation, and if you cancel without 48
hours' notice, we charge a $250 inconvenience fee."

HOW TO EAT COOL

An Idiot's Guide to Dining in Pretentious Restaurants

For many, many diners these days, what you eat isn't nearly as important as what you look like while eating it, who sees you, and where you're eating it. Should you so desire to step into their stilettos for an evening, a few pointers:

1. Arrive late.

2. When you get to your table, ask for a different one.
   Or at *least* demand one by the window from the get-go.

3. When you're finally seated, look bored.
   Yawn a lot. Twirl your hair with your fingers.

4. Whether you're dining alone or not, repeatedly check voice mail on your cell phone.

5. Order only those things on the menu that you've never heard of and that have at least a four-sentence description beneath them.

6. Continue looking bored until your appetizer arrives. If the wine comes first, be sure to send the first bottle back.

7. When the entrées arrive, sneer at the server for interrupting your call.

· ·

YOUR EATIN' HEART:
MORE THAN JUST NOURISHMENT

Food signifies more than mere sustenance. Too often, it's considered the enemy. Too bad we can't just enjoy it for what it is—an outlet for artistic expression, pleasure, and fuel for our bodies. So the next time you gorge thoughtlessly on donuts, remember that food is your friend. The relationship you have with it is up to you.

is for

FUNDAMENTALS

fun • da • ment • als
\fən-də-'men-təlz\
n. **1.** An original or generating source related to essential structure, function, or facts. **2.** The basics. The skinny. **3.** Those things without which one is generally pretty screwed.

SO YOU'VE
BEEN READING
THIS BOOK.

(And you're just so loving it.) So far, you've gotten a brief overview of a lot of essential (and not so essential) things. (And, golly, you're only up to F.)

But maybe you're looking for something more concise: a quick rundown of how to live better, more effectively. (A *Bluffer's Guide* to life, so to speak.) That's where Fundamentals comes in. Think of this chapter as a graduate degree in philosophy, logic, human behavior, and time management—tossed into a blender and zapped in the microwave.

Sometimes you want limitless options. (Especially when assembling sundaes. Or picking your next vacation.) But sometimes, nothing works better than a streamlined plan. (The perfect ten-piece wardrobe. A three-step skin-care routine. The complete Modern Library.) So, with that in mind, we've come up with a few principles, ideas, tips, and what-have-you's to make it all a little easier.

Herewith, in no particular order (which is how it should be), the DailyCandy Fundamentals:

TIP WELL.

COROLLARY
Be generally generous.

CALL YOUR PARENTS.

CALL YOUR GRANDPARENTS.

SWEAT THE SMALL STUFF.
DRINK LOTS OF WATER.
DRINK LOTS OF WINE.
WRITE THANK-YOU NOTES.

PAY ATTENTION TO THE EXTREMITIES:
GOOD HAIR, NAILS, AND SHOES MAKE ALL THE DIFFERENCE.

INDULGE IN THE EXTREME.
BALANCE IS OVERRATED.

WASH BEHIND YOUR EARS.

Choose to be happy.

NEVER CLIP YOUR NAILS IN PUBLIC.

ACKNOWLEDGE GOOD WORK WHEREVER YOU FIND IT.

FLOSS.

THINGS YOU CAN BUY ON THE CHEAP
without noticing a huge difference:

IBUPROFEN
CANNED TOMATOES
PEPPER
COFFEE FILTERS
FLIP-FLOPS
BLEACH

THINGS YOU CAN'T BUY ON THE CHEAP
without noticing a huge difference:

SHOES
SUSHI
WINE
PRODUCE
BRAS
STATIONERY

KEEP A DIARY.

IT'S AMAZING THE
DETAILS YOU'LL FORGET
WITHIN A FEW MONTHS.

CAVEAT:

*If you keep a diary,
it will be read.*

COROLLARY:

*There are two kinds of
people—diary writers
and diary readers.*

BAD DRIVERS DESERVE TO BE SHOT.

DO SOMETHING THAT SCARES YOU.

THEN DO SOMETHING
ELSE THAT SCARES YOU.

FIND YOUR MORAL COMPASS.

*And on a regular basis, do whatever you need to
do to realign it. (Religion, exercise, meditation, AA, yoga,
bungee-jumping.) Because that's the thing about your
moral compass: It will, from time to time, get knocked out of whack.*

MOVE ON.

YOU'LL NEVER GET ANYWHERE ARGUING:

POLITICS

RELIGION

CHILD-REARING

BUT YOU MIGHT MAKE HEADWAY DEBATING:

DIETS

DINNER

DATING

*Sometimes you need to direct your life.
And sometimes you need
to react to what life directs at you.*

IF YOU HEAR A
COMPLIMENT
ABOUT A FRIEND,
PASS IT ALONG.

EAT ONE SERVING OF BRIGHTLY COLORED FOOD DAILY.

COLORS SHOULD BE THOSE NORMALLY OCCURRING IN NATURE.

(Which means orange cheese-puffs don't count.)

LITTLE KIDS ARE WISE. LISTEN TO THEM.

THE FOUR BEST FOUR-WORD PHRASES IN THE ENGLISH LANGUAGE:

1. WANT TO COME IN?
2. IT'S ON THE HOUSE.
3. YOU LOOK SO YOUNG.
4. SHUT THE FUCK UP.

THE THREE BEST THREE-WORD PHRASES IN THE ENGLISH LANGUAGE:

1. I LOVE YOU.
2. YOU WERE RIGHT.
3. THAT WAS DELICIOUS!

THE TWO BEST TWO-WORD PHRASES IN THE ENGLISH LANGUAGE:

1. I'M SORRY.
2. SNOW DAY!

THE SINGLE BEST WORD:

1. NO.

Dance, if only in your underpants and around your living room, at least twice per week. Feel free to sing while you're at it (especially songs from The Sound of Music*).*

IF YOU WERE MEANT TO BE TOGETHER, YOU WOULD BE TOGETHER.

NAP.

BUY YOURSELF FLOWERS.

WISH ON PENNIES AND STARS.

MULTITASK
(LEG LIFTS IN FRONT OF THE TV WORK WELL).

So what are we saying? That you should have a code. It might be all of these things, it might be some of them, or others we haven't included here. But once you've developed your code, stick by it. Like your own Jiminy Cricket, let it be your guide. Then, when situations don't feel right, you'll know why and you'll know what to do. And won't it be nice to have the guesswork taken out of that?

is for

GIRLS & GUYS

girls and guys \gərlz ənd gīz\ *n, pl.* **1.** Slang terms for women and men. **2.** Often used to describe casual gatherings of friends, when said gathering includes a mingling of the genders. *(Girls and guys, are were ready to play spin the bottle?)* **3.** The PG-13 and potentially R-rated version of "girls and boys."

WHO'S FROM MARS? WHO'S FROM VENUS?

Who actually paid hard-earned cash for such a stupidly titled book? Sure, girls probably care a little more about handbags and shoes than guys do. But that's not the same as being more vain. Because when it comes to vanity, the score is even-steven.

All of which got us thinking about the difference between girls and guys. And goodness if that isn't a fascinating subject. Philosophers have been debating it since Eve ruined Adam's paradise. (Could she help it if she was the smarter of the two?)

So we settle, once and for all, the difference between the sexes—not with some detailed, cross-referenced, biohistorical, anthropological hagiography, but rather with a simple—perhaps reductionist—list. Which, let's face it, is as much as the human pea-brain can handle when trying to figure this stuff out.*

*Every coin has two sides; so disagree all you like—all of this is just food for thought.

 **Girls** | **Guys**

Girls	Guys
SWEET	SALTY
OPRAH	CHRIS MOYLES
BOTTLED WATER	FROM THE TAP
STYLIST	BARBER
SIP	CHUG
SQUAT	STAND
PEEPING THONG	PLUMBER'S SMILE
EVIAN	BIG GULP
ELLIPTICAL	FREE WEIGHTS
BOTTOM	TOP
WAX	SHAVE
PAGE SIX	PAGE THREE
DESPERATE HOUSEWIVES	*ENTOURAGE*
FRISÉE	ICEBERG
CHEESE	CRACKERS
ACTORS	ATHLETES
EYES	CARNAL KNOWLEDGE
SCARLET	RED
MAGENTA	RED
ROSE	RED

VIOLET	PURPLE-RED
RUBY	RED
LAVENDER	PURPLE
DANDELION	YELLOW
GRILLED	FRIED
PUGS	BULLDOGS
BATH	SHOWER
SPA	GOLF
HEAT	*FHM*
ANGELINA JOLIE	ANGELINA JOLIE
I'LL HAVE A DECAF SOY LATTE.	A CUP OF COFFEE, PLEASE.
BRAVE IN THE FACE OF PAIN	UTTER WIMPS
I HAVE A COLD. IT'S NOTHING.	I'M DYING.
DIET COKE	FAT COKE
INSOMNIA	NARCOLEPSY
SINATRA	DINO
NAG	AVOID
ZIG	ZAG
LAUNDRY	DISHES
I LOOK FAT.	BABY, YOU DON'T LOOK FAT.

is for
HOME

 **home** \'hōm\ *n.* **1.** Where one lives; a residence. **2.** An environment offering security and happiness. **3.** The place one goes to escape the world outside. *(Dude, this party sucks. I'm going* home.*)* **4.** The blank canvas for people's design sensibility, both the wonderful and the horrific. **5.** See also: crib, crash pad, nest, digs.

THE GOOD NEWS IS THAT HOME IS WHERE THE HEART IS.

The bad news, in your case, is that it's also where the circa-1993 hot-pink couch, *Cribs*-inspired zebra-skin rug, and twelve-dollar map-of-the-world shower curtain are.

Why is it that you can dress like a champ, but when it comes to outfitting your pad you're hopeless?

The truth is it doesn't take wads of money to make a house feel like a home. If you can clothe yourself with style, you can decorate, as well. Take that ugly chair you hate and get it reupholstered. Bitch-slap your carpet out the door and let the floor go bare. If you wouldn't wear it, don't try to live in it. Just remember: From your first forays into Barbie Dream House decor to those post-graduation cinderblocks, you've been teaching yourself interior design all your life. Now all you need are a few pointers.

Oh. Right-o, the "I'm just renting" excuse.

GETTING YOUR FIX
Cheap-o Apartment Fixes

You took the time to decorate your college digs with pictures of Damon Albarn, and you didn't even plan to stay in that purgatorial space for a full year. Here are some quick home fixes that take about as long as a mani-pedi.

IS THAT A TUBE OF CAULK, OR ARE YOU JUST HAPPY TO SEE US? A fresh toothpaste-like tube of caulk—the white stuff that seals between your bath tiles—costs less than a tenner. Chip out the old moldy stuff with a utility knife (wear glasses or goggles so you don't get it in your eyes). Clean the blech with bleach. Squeeze the caulk in to the crack (sorry, there's no way to say this without bad puns), and run your finger over it to make it smooth. Let it dry for twenty-four hours. By the way, you can thank us for the oh-so-satisfying sensation of caulk-smoothing later. It could be the best action you're going to see in that bath all year.

WATER DAMAGE: Exposed water heater? Hang a closet rod in front of it (make sure it's far enough away that you don't risk fire) and hang a cute curtain.

NAIL IT: When short of spackle, fill nail holes with toothpaste, let dry, and smile.

GROUT OF THIS WORLD: Cleaning stained grout between tiles requires only two things: bleach and a toothbrush. But don't wear your favorite Missoni because bleach, well, bleaches.

GOING TO POT: Potted flowers at your doorstep or in a window box (there are ones you can hang right over the ledge; no screws required) gives even a room with no view some charm. Fill them with annuals, herbs, ivy, or whatever strikes your fancy.

KITCHEN CONFIDENTIAL: All you need to change drawer pulls and handles is a screwdriver. Stainless steel ones cost the same as a bottle of Thunderbird. Also, try easy-to-install and later-take-them-with-you Flor carpet tiles to cover that icky yellow vinyl floor.

CURTAINS FOR YOU: Make too-long curtains fit-to-size by shortening them with hem tape that binds by ironing.

CHALK IT UP: You've seen the chalkboard-paint trend, but what about painting the inside of your front door? It's a great place to leave reminders and love notes to your babycakes.

HONEY, I'M HOME!
How Do You Know You're Home?

I know it's pathetic and cat-person-y, but I don't care:
My cat meets me at the door. Wherever Hobson is, that's home.
LOLA, 34

When I kick off my shoes, turn on the TV, and see the many, many
reruns of *Aqua Teen Hunger Force* saved on my TiVo.
SIMON, 29

My flatmate always welcomes me with a hearty,
"There you are! Been whoring around again?"
Then we make gin and tonics and listen to records.
Does home get better than that?
JEN, 27

The smell of yellow mustard. Gross, I know.
And if you had told me ten years ago that I'd associate that smell
with anything good I probably would've
decked you. But it's my husband's favorite condiment, and so for
better or worse (literally), it's the smell of home.
MADGE, 42

My bed. It's the only thing I really splurged on, from
the pillow-top mattress to the 600-thread-count
Egyptian cotton sheets. But it was worth it. No fancy hotel
room bed can even come close.
VIV, 30

My welcome mat. It says, "Go Away."
VIOLET, 33

They don't call them experts for nothing.

NAME-DROPPING:
DESIGN MAVEN MATCH-UP

Match the quote or fact to the guru, then impress at your next design snob to-do.

1. "TAKE YOUR PLEASURE SERIOUSLY."	A. LUDWIG MIES VAN DER ROHE
2. DESIGNED HIS OWN COFFIN.	B. CONSTANCE SPRY
3. "PERHAPS BELIEVING IN GOOD DESIGN IS LIKE BELIEVING IN GOD —IT MAKES YOU AN OPTIMIST."	C. DAVID HICKS
4. TAUGHT THE MASSES TO DECORATE WITH GARDEN FLOWERS.	D. COCO CHANEL
5. "I DON'T WANT TO BE INTERESTING. I WANT TO BE GOOD."	E. CHARLES EAMES
6. REARRANGES THE FURNITURE IN HER HOTEL ROOM.	F. KELLY WEARSTLER
7. "FASHION IS ARCHITECTURE, IT'S A MATTER OF PROPORTIONS."	G. SIR TERENCE CONRAN

ANSWERS: 1E; 2C; 3G; 4B; 5A; 6F; 7D

Be it ever so humble, there's no place like Homebase. Words to live by? Perhaps not. But it's important to remember that beautifying your home, whether with big-time overhauls or minor touches, is always within reach if you're willing to use imagination and effort. Moreover, it often has less to do with what you've bought than what you do with the pieces you have. Sometimes, all it takes is a scented candle and your favorite CD to make a place feel homey; other times, all you really need is to sleep in your own bed—dirty sheets, crappy mattress, and all.

is for
INTIMACY

in • ti • ma • cy \'in-tə-mə-sē\
n. **1.** The condition of being intimate. **2.** The condition of being
involved with someone in a roman-
tic, passionate, and often frustrating manner. *(It's the
irony of* intimacy *that someone who drives me so crazy
can drive me so crazy.)* **3.** The kind of closeness with
a romantic partner that is typically marked by equal
parts tension, panic, and bliss.

SOME PEOPLE CLAIM THAT RELATIONSHIPS ARE EASY. They don't get jealous. They don't fight about blowing the rent on a pair of shoes. And they have mind-blowing sex every night.

Some people also lie.

Intimate relationships are complex, infuriating, and glorious. When they're bad, you're arguing about the thermostat and who's restocking the toilet paper. When they're good, you end up with someone who loves you even when you've been possessed by a stomach flu. (And somewhere in the middle, there's make-up sex.)

On the following pages, we'll explore the craziness of relationships, from the secret language of e-mail and the upside of rejection to knowing when to discuss and when to shut up. If you forget everything else you're about to read, remember this: When it comes to intimacy, a little humility goes a long way.

Before you get into it, it's best to know what you're dealing with.
Because once you know your quarry, you'll be successful in its pursuit. And though we're talking in
terms of opposite sex, you can substitute the female equivalent to the same effect.

MEN A Field Guide

TYPE A: THE SPVIP
(THE SELF-PROCLAIMED VIP)

CHARACTER TRAITS: Witty, urbane, charming, laugh-out-loud funny. Commonly found at the center of attention. Possesses an edge so intoxicating that it doesn't matter what he looks like.

THE LOOK: Black stylish shirt. Vintage trainers. Cool jeans.

APPROACH: Make a joke about wanting to buy him a drink so he can entertain you. Let him ask you for your number. The key is to show detachment—and stroke his ego. Repeatedly.

• •

TYPE B: THE MODEL

CHARACTER TRAITS: Extremely insecure about brains-to-beauty ratio. Looks too beautiful to date mere mortals, but is often the nicest breed and easiest to land.

THE LOOK: Tall, lean—with glowing complexion and tresses he loves to play with. Wears tattered Levi's, white T-shirt, and hooded sweatshirt. Never wears a hat.

APPROACH: Inquire about his latest diet and throw in scientific terminology (feel free to make up words—he'll never know). Engage with witty banter. Tell him to e-mail you because you'd love to pick his brain for a work project over coffee sometime.

TYPE C: THE HEDGE FUNDAMENTALIST

CHARACTER TRAITS: Handsome, groomed, dressed for success. All about the entrance. Wants to be seen with the hottest date, yet secretly desires a partner with more brains. Often leaves the party alone.

THE LOOK: Preppy. Ralph Lauren, Tod's loafers, aviator sunglasses.

APPROACH: If you're upfront, he'll think you're a vixen. Write your number on a napkin. He can show it off to his friends.

• •

TYPE D: HOLLYWOOD SCHMOOZER

CHARACTER TRAITS: Ever the social chameleon, he throws himself into whatever glittery crowd he's trying to impress.

THE LOOK: Short. Depressingly so. Arrogant. Talks too loud. Baggy jeans, retro Nikes, spiky hair. Umbilically attached to his BlackBerry.

APPROACH: Short and brief: He's ADD. And armed with distracting gadgets.

• •

TYPE E: MAN OF LETTERS

CHARACTER TRAITS: Literary, complex, mysterious. The only thing he'll want to play is Shakespeare.

THE LOOK: Jeans or cords with Converse One Stars.

APPROACH: Pull up a chair next to him and enlist him to help keep those stupid, drunk, rugger-bugger types away.

• •

TYPE F: MR. OFFICE SPACE

CHARACTER TRAITS: If not already married to his sixth-form sweetie, he's looking for a wife. He's not a workaholic: His real passions are sports, beer, and his mother. In that order.

THE LOOK: Totally normal. Khaki pants, white button-down, deck shoes.

APPROACH: Casual conversation. He's all about ball-busters (Oedipal complex, anyone?) and will follow your lead.

MEN AND MANNERS

Approach paramours the way you would anything else in life: Be yourself. Remember *The Rules*? For a while there, that silly husband-snaring book written by two women (one of whom got divorced, *ahem*) convinced women to wear lipstick to the gym, decline any invitation not issued at least five days in advance, never split the check, and never initiate sex. Who would ever want to be with such an ungracious creature?

So what are the new rules?

RULE #1: There are no rules. If there was a foolproof method for falling in love, then why are so many people still looking? And consider what a bore the whole commitment process would be if everybody called at the perfect time, said the right things, and didn't kiss you for a month.

RULE #2: Always offer to split the bill. Happy universal fact: Women make money, too. So be willing to pay your share. The era of using dates as meal tickets is over. The best plan? Take turns treating. It's sexier than going Dutch.

RULE #3: Wear sexy lingerie. As if anyone could feel attractive in sagging undies. Who do you think you're kidding?

RULE #4: BYOT. (Bring your own toothbrush.) You never know where the night may take you, and you never want someone to suggest you might want some floss or chewing gum.

RULE #5: Send proper thank-you notes. It happens so often that two people share the same evening and walk away with two different experiences. The best way to make sure you both are on the same page is with the morning-after e-mail. For example:

TEMPLATE: THE "THANK HEAVENS!" E-MAIL

To: Him
From: You

Message:
Had so much fun. Would love to do it again . . .
u around? Speak soon.

TEMPLATE: THE "THANKS, BUT, UM, NO THANKS!" E-MAIL

To: Him
From: You

Message:
Thanks for the lovely date. I really want you to meet
a friend of mine. Will be in touch. Take care.

**TEMPLATE: THE "THANKS FOR THE LOVELY DATE, BUT . . .
SEE YA!" E-MAIL**

To: Him
From: You

Message:
Strangest thing happened after our date.
My boss called me and offered me an amazing promotion
in Paris. I'm leaving tomorrow. Au revoir!

You meet. You date. Two months later, you realize
you're seriously "in like." Anxiety creeps in and perspective checks out.
Before initiating the "what are we?" dialogue,
it's important to see which direction the relationship is heading.

READING
THE SIGNS:

HE LIKES YOU IF HE . . .

1. Gives. Gives. Gives.
   (And not necessarily in the financial sense.)

2. Is interested in hearing how you are. Really.

3. Remembers your mum's name.

4. Assumes you're spending the weekend together.

STOP CALLING WHEN HE . . .

1. Repeatedly sends text messages rather than calling.

2. Admits he doesn't love animals.

3. Signs you up for a gym membership.

4. Forgets to trim his nose hairs.

5. Has a dress hanging in his closet. (Either belonging to him
   or someone else. Either way, not a promising sign.)

THE SECRET LANGUAGE OF RESPONSE TIME ON E-MAIL . . .

1. IMMEDIATE (within two minutes): Polite and quick.

2. TWO HOURS: Strong time-management skills.

3. ONE DAY: Trying hard to write the perfect message.

4. TWO DAYS: On the fence. Or slammed with work.

5. A WEEK OR MORE: Technically challenged.

6. NEVER: Inexcusable.

GOING BLIND

To Blind Date or Not to Blind Date?

There is no right or wrong answer. But there is one overarching principle: Trust your source. Herewith, an answering machine postmortem left by one girl who forgot to check the references.

"Do not go on a blind date. Just don't. Unless you get validation from a third party. And I don't think mothers, aunts, and my dentist count as third parties. It's got to be an independent third party who is not the yenta—new rule. He was a dud. A total, total dud. And yes, he has brown hair. But he neglected to say that he has, like, no hair. So that's it. Call me so I can tell you about the snorting problem. He was so not worth a new pair of fishnets."

Say It with Flowers

SO HE SENT FLOWERS. WHAT DO HIS BLOOMS SAY?

RED ROSES
Classic, but demonstrates minimal creativity.

TULIPS
The chap has class. Extra brownie points for French tulips.

ONE ORCHID
Trying really, really hard. And you respect him for it.

CALLA LILIES
He talked to some friends and got good advice.

PEONIES
He's a mama's boy. And he's learned well.

GERBERA DAISIES
Sweet.

CARNATIONS
Dump him.

BABY'S BREATH
Why did you go out with him in the first place?

By the way, a lady should always return the favor. How? With a cool plant, like a scented geranium. Not only will he be shocked by the gift, but he'll be fascinated by this wild living thing in his flat. (Which paves the way for . . . you!)

It's as emotionally draining to break up as it is to move in together.
Both involve rejection ("My taste does not suck!"), life overhauls ("I'm cutting off all my hair!"), and
proper etiquette ("How can I politely tell him I never want to see his rodent-like face again?").

MEN BEHAVING BADLY; GIRLS GOING WILD
Breaking Up with Dignity

In fairness, breaking up sucks for everyone. How to do it without incurring a lifetime of bad karma?

1. GET IT OVER WITH QUICKLY. Instead of trying to manipulate the other person into thinking he or she is the one ending it, just be honest. The longer you stay together, the worse it gets. Duh.

2. BEAUTY IS IN THE EYES. Let's be honest: Looks matter. Doesn't matter how universally beautiful a person may be. If you aren't turned on by them, it's hard to be with them. You just can't admit it's about looks, so pull out the white lie. You love hanging out with them, but don't feel the passion.

3. AVOID CLICHÉS. "It's not you, it's me." "I don't deserve you." You know the lines. They're all a load of crap.

4. MEET FACE-TO-FACE. Never put it in writing or say it into an answering machine. (These things get passed around.) Meet in a discreet location where you won't be embarrassed to cry. And take two cars, so that when you leave, you can literally go your separate ways.

5. GIVE FEEDBACK GENTLY. It's over. May as well learn something from it. Tell them when you started falling out of love and lust, explain the signs you tried to use, and what you were thinking of before doing it. This is painful, but is the only way to move from lovers to friends. (See sidebar.)

6. DON'T CALL OR E-MAIL. You dumped him. Give him space to recoup. And if you're wondering about that T-shirt you left at his place, well, give him that, too.

HE SAYS
YOU SPEND
TOO MUCH?

Not only does living together mean you'll see each other at your worst, but it also means seeing the evidence: shopping bags, tampon wrappers, credit card bills. When he brings up your spending habit, be prepared with some good comebacks.

ONE

"I'm stimulating the economy."

TWO

"That's not mine. It's my sister's."

THREE

"So what? You're not paying for it."

FOUR

"What else was I going to do when you were golfing?"

FIVE

"These shoes? They're not new. I wear them all the time. You've never noticed???"

LET'S BE FRIENDS?

Trying to form a platonic friendship with someone with whom you've been intimately involved is quite the feat. It rarely works. How do you know if you can really be friends?

You don't sleep together. If you're hooking up, then one of you still has feelings.

You play matchmaker for each other. And can double date without getting jealous.

The way he holds his fork doesn't make you crazy. Meaning you didn't end the relationship in disgust and can sit through dinner without losing your mind.

Is He the One?

ONE **DRAW A PICTURE OF YOUR BELOVED.** TWO **CAN YOU IMAGINE KISSING YOUR LOVED ONE IF HE HAD NO TEETH?** THREE **DO YOU TRUST HIM WITH YOUR SAVINGS ACCOUNT?** FOUR **DOES HE KNOW HOW TO LAUGH AT HIMSELF?** FIVE **IS TRAVELING WITH HIM FUN?** SIX **DOES HE CHALLENGE YOU?** SEVEN **DO YOU CONSIDER HIM FAMILY?** EIGHT **ARE YOU SURE HE WANTS TO GET MARRIED?** NINE **MARRIAGE, KIDS, MORTGAGE, AND DAY CARE. ARE YOU SCARED?**

FULLY ENGAGED

Everyone will be showering you with false advice and plain old lies.

1. "Don't get married. Enjoy your time being engaged." Such crap.
   No one should plan a wedding for more than six months.
   The longer you wait, the less excited you'll be.

2. "The wedding is a reflection of the couple." Rarely.
   It caters to the parents. Or whoever pays the bill.

3. "You don't have to have a bridal shower."
   Try telling that to Aunt Sally when she's in guilt mode.

4. "Your mother and father can't wait to help you with planning."
   One word: disaster.

A TABLE
FOR ONE,
PLEASE
Traveling Life Alone

While the joy of finding a lifelong partner to laugh at life with you makes the ride a lot better, it's in no way a means to find yourself. In truth, learning to love and to laugh at your quirks and offbeat nature begins with you. Before anyone else can love your freaky self, you have to.

is for

JET-SETTING

jet-sett • ing
\'jet-se-tin\
v. **1.** Archaic: The activities of an international social set made up of those who travel from one fashionable place to another. *(Jackie O. and Ari, the consummate* jet-setters, *used to party it up in Capri in the late '60s.)* **2.** Being swank in a location that is not one's primary residence. **3.** Traveling, taking off, getting away from it all—on grand (or not so grand) scales.

IF LIFE WERE FAIR,

you'd be able to hop the next flight to Marrakech or spend the weekend in Ibiza. But then you'd probably be too busy to read this fascinating chapter, which is all about being a jet-setter—no matter what your means or situation in life.

We won't get into the folding-versus-rolling packing debate; we won't tell you which European resort is the most likely place for you to run into whatever hotshot celebrity; and we definitely won't give you an exhaustive tour of Western Europe (for that, you really must read DailyCandy's travel edition). Rather, we'll tell you how to make the most of your travels, wherever they take you.

Travel Lexicon

We know more than a couple of words have come to mind while traveling. And they all seem to have four letters. DailyCandy feels your pain, so we'd like to give you a few to replace the ones you just can't say out loud.

scary-on *n.* An item that's clearly too big to fit into a plane's overhead compartment, whose owner insists on carrying it on, anyway.

heirport *n.* On-the-spot airport created in a remote location to accommodate a private plane carrying passengers on route to seasonal home. *(Our new island is days away from the nearest commercial landing strip, which means we'll just have to use Daddy's heirport to land the jet.)*

frequent liar *n.* Someone who boasts incessantly about traveling to places he/she has never been.

screamese *n.* The loud voice used only to speak to foreigners. *(Rather than learn a few rudimentary terms in Spanish, Harold preferred to ask for directions in Screamese.)*

business ass *n.* The dude who shows up at the airport in his best suit thinking it will help him get an upgrade.

For all anyone knows, you could have a Priceline ticket to Peoria.
But look and act the part of the glamorous traveler and you'll not only get treated better,
you'll feel better. At least until you get to Peoria.

DRESSING DOWN, LIVING LARGE

Assembling Your Travel Look

Think you're pulling off the whole shabby-rich-person look? Newsflash: Very few can pull that off. Here are a few tips for looking like a seasoned traveler.

1. LAYER, LAYER, LAYER. One minute you're drenched in sweat, the next you're shivering like a shaved Chihuahua on the tundra. The menopause? More like a fourteen-hour flight with a wonky thermostat. For tops, three layers is standard (a tank, warm jumper, and a wrap that can double as a blanket). For bottoms, comfortable trousers are best.

2. ACCESSORIZE—BUT NOT TOO MUCH. Wear your signature jewelry only—that necklace from Dad, a wedding, engagement, or favorite ring. Dangly, bulky, or complicated accessories look gaudy—plus, they just get tangled up in everything and make unwanted noise.

3. DE-FUZZIFY. A rolling stone may gather no moss, but even the most stylish traveler gathers tons of lint. Forgot your lint brush? Look for a FedEx center and use one of their sticky-backed clear pouches to rid yourself of fuzz.

4. MAKEUP ESSENTIALS. Minimal makeup is key for the jet-setter. Concealer, mascara, and a moisturizing lip gloss are all ideal. Also, bring a mini spray bottle of Evian to hydrate your face.

5. PERFUME. Just a touch of something classic—Chanel No. 5, perhaps. But not too much—you don't want to overpower your fellow passengers.

6. NO TRACKSUITS. Ever.

YOU CAN TAKE IT WITH YOU

Sure, it's important to pack light, but smart travelers agree:
Some things just can't be left behind. Here are the top ten things
we suggest you never leave home without:

1. EARPLUGS. When is the last time you actually heard something pleasant on an airplane? 2. NOISE-CANCELING HEADPHONES. Ditto. 3. SLEEP MASK. A wearable do-not-disturb sign. 4. TRAVEL LAUNDRY KIT. Cleanliness is next to godliness—even on vacation. 5. CONVERTERS, TRANSFORMERS, OR PLUG ADAPTORS. 6. MINI FIRST-AID KIT. For all of life's little accidents. 7. SWISS ARMY KNIFE. As useful now as ever. (Just don't try carrying it on.) 8. UMBRELLA. 9. MOIST TOWELETTES. Because you hope for the best, but should be prepared for the worst. 10. TRAVEL CANDLES. Some hotels smell glorious. Others do not. And rarely do the windows open.

*Remember that trip when Sadie McPushypants got herself an upgrade to first class
while you played the role of burp cloth to your pint-sized seatmate?
Or the time that "romantic getaway" turned into "the worst breakup of all time"?
Let's make sure that never happens again.*

MAKING
THE UPGRADE
How to Escape Coach Class

The plane is packed. Your nerves are shot. Ready to trade stale peanuts in coach for in-flight manicures in business? Getting an upgrade may be harder than ever, but it's not impossible. A few tricks of the trade:

GO THE EXTRA MILE What are you saving your frequent-flier miles for? Don't kid yourself—you'll never take that trip to Yemen. The number of miles required for an upgrade can vary from 15,000 to 180,000, depending on carrier and destination, but the higher your status, the better your chances. So stay brand loyal and use alliance and codeshare partners. If you don't have the miles, you can buy them to top off your account.

CLASS SYSTEM The cheaper your ticket, the tougher the upgrade. Y and B coach fares are pricier and more flexible. (Letters vary, so check when you buy.) When purchasing your ticket, ask about an upgrade—some are available in advance. Most airlines won't give up business class seats until the day of travel, but they'll note your request in the computer, and persistence can pay off. (Of course, it could also make them hate you, so mind your manners.) Preferred customers get confirmed faster—three to seven days before flight time for elite status, the same day for a regular flier.

PLANE ENGLISH For the most bang for the mileage buck, fly midday or pick long-haul flights. (Larger planes have more seats in every class. Duh.) Check the model before you buy your ticket on www.seatguru.com or the carrier's sites. In general, 747s, 767s, 777s, and Airbus 330/340s are all good bets. Shorter flights and smaller planes just aren't worth the hassle. Unless you are on a 737-800 or a 737-900, all you'll get is a few extra cashews.

WEEKEND WARRIORS Everyone (and his agent) wants a flatbed seat on Sunday's LAX–JFK red-eye. Improve your upgrade odds by flying less-trafficked days like Tuesday, Wednesday, and Saturday. Thursday, Friday, and Sunday are when full-fare business-class travelers fly. And their superstar status trumps whatever you've got.

SPEAKING OF AGENTS It may not pay to DIY. A savvy travel agent can score deeply discounted long-haul business class tickets with a fifty-day advance purchase. Prices could end up competitive with coach fares.

AIR-STYLES OF THE RICH AND FAMOUS Need further incentive to live large in flight? On Singapore Airlines you can preorder dinner (lobster thermidor, rack of lamb), lounge in Givenchy PJs, and pen your wish-you-were-heres on fancy stationery. Virgin Atlantic offers door-to-door car service (leaving more time for the chic Upper Class bar). The film library on Qantas includes more than fifty flicks.

COME FLY

WITH ME?

Congratulations! You're finally considering your first vacation together (as a couple, a quasi-couple, whatever). Here's a little questionnaire you can give your sweetie to help you determine whether you're ready to take to the skies together.

1. HYPOTHETICAL SCENARIO:
One of us gets bumped to first class. Who's going —you or me?

2. COMPLETE THE FOLLOWING: WHEN IN ROME

A) get wasted, dude!

B) don't miss the Spanish Steps.

C) check out those hot Italian chicks.

D) beware of panhandlers.

3. I HAVE SOME EXTRA ROOM IN MY SUITCASE. I SHOULD PACK:

A) running shoes.

B) some candles to put by the tub.

C) your handcuffs.

D) my handcuffs.

(Trick question. There is no way I'll have extra room in my suitcase, fool.)

4. COMPLETE THE FOLLOWING— GUIDEBOOKS ARE:

A) useful, but shouldn't be relied upon.

B) to be used in conjunction with highlighters.

C) for tourists, not travelers.

D) best used as a doorstop.

5. YOU'VE FINALLY AGREED TO TAKE ME TO YOUR PARENTS' HOUSE FOR A LONG WEEKEND. WE GET THERE AND YOU:

A) introduce me to your parents, then leave me with your mother for some quality time.

B) suggest that you get the bags while I get to know your parents.

C) have your parents give me a tour of the house while you play with Rex, the family dog.

D) do not dream of leaving me alone with your parents for even one second.

6. TRUE OR FALSE:
France, like any foreign country, is a place where you should be careful not to eat too much.

(False. You tell me not to eat in France, it's over.)

7. WHAT EXACTLY IS YOUR POLICY ON CARRYING OTHER PEOPLE'S LUGGAGE?

8. WE'RE AT THE AIRPORT AND ONE OF US (I.E., ME) GETS HUNGRY. YOU THEN:

A) tell me you'll watch the bags and send me to the nearest Pizza Hut.

B) ask me what I'm in the mood for and go looking for it.

C) suggest we find a nice place to eat, since we have forty-five minutes before boarding.

D) take something sweet out of your pocket, because you knew I'd be hungry and that airport food is awful.

9. WE GET SEPARATED. WE'LL FIND EACH OTHER AT:

A) the nearest sports bar.

B) the nearest boutique hotel.

C) the nearest shoe store.

10. DO YOU HAVE A FETISH FOR HAVING SEX IN HISTORICAL LANDMARKS OR NATIONAL PARKS?

11. FILL IN THE BLANK:
When we get on the plane, your iPod is _____ iPod.

12. I WILL NOT UNDER ANY CIRCUMSTANCES TRY TO GET A LOOK AT YOUR PASSPORT PHOTO.

_____

(sign here)

• •

WHEREVER YOU GO,
THERE YOU ARE.

Dorothy, that quintessential jet-setter (she flew a *house* into another *dimension*), returned with one simple conviction: There's no place like home. Her point? Our travels are only great insofar as they teach us to understand the value of home—or, as T.S. Eliot said, "to arrive where we began, and to know it for the first time." Whatever that means.

is for
KIN

kin \'kin\ *n.* **1.** Relatives; family. **2.** The people who expect you to keep in touch on a semi-regular basis, if only so they can accuse you of never calling. **3.** The assortment of alarmingly incompatible people one is forced to converse with on major holidays.

TOLSTOY, THAT OLD QUIPPER OF YORE,

claimed that all happy families are the same, while all unhappy families are unhappy in their own way. (Not exactly a glass-half-full kind of guy, that Tolstoy.) The truth, of course, is that most families aren't all happy or unhappy, but, like people themselves, have ups and downs, good days (Mum got a promotion!) and bad days (Tim Jr. crashed the car!). Sure, they're the people who molded you into the magnificent specimen you are today. They're also the reason you're in therapy, are single with a dog at age thirty-five, and dread the month of December.

But pretending they don't exist isn't an option. (Not a healthy one, anyway.) So in this chapter, we'll delve into the world of how to handle sibling rivalry, survive family reunions, pick your battles, and finally understand what the hell your mother is talking about.

The world of parenting sure has changed. Heather has two mommies; Jake's had four daddies; Marla was raised by her nanny; and Simon's folks haven't spoken in years. But whatever form they've taken, conventional or otherwise, your parents are your parents. They brought you into the world, after all.

THE MOTHER
TRANSLATOR

Her martyrdom is instinctual, her wires permanently crossed, and her passive-aggressive moves as well-rehearsed as a Bolshoi ballerina's. If she said what she meant, you wouldn't recognize her. So we present you with an official guide to reading between the lines.

WHAT SHE SAYS: "So that's the blouse you're going with?"

WHAT SHE MEANS: "You look like a whore on the streets of Calcutta."

WHAT SHE SAYS: "Have you heard from that boy you had a date with last Friday?"

WHAT SHE MEANS: "Did you put out too soon and scare him off?"

WHAT SHE SAYS: "I can't find my diamond studs anywhere."

WHAT SHE MEANS: "Give them back, you thieving ingrate."

WHAT SHE SAYS: "You look happy!"

WHAT SHE MEANS: "Get your ass on a diet, you fat tub of goo."

WHAT SHE SAYS: "Is that the new hairstyle in California?"

WHAT SHE MEANS: "Did a leprous badger climb atop your head and die?"

WHAT SHE SAYS: "You're our little career girl!"

WHAT SHE MEANS: "Your ovaries are shriveling as we speak!"

WHAT SHE SAYS: "I know you've been busy."

WHAT SHE MEANS: "You have heartlessly abandoned the woman who gave you life and left her to suffer the indignities of old age alone. You haven't even asked me how my knee is feeling. Not very good, as a matter of fact—it was humid yesterday. Oh, and the showerhead in the upstairs bathroom broke, plus Dad's sleep apnea kept me up all night. Not that you care."

There's nothing quite as odd as sibling relationships.
You may have absolutely nothing in common, yet still share a bond.
You're forced together in conditions not of your choosing,
are often required to share a room or toilet,
and usually know way too much about each other.

OH, BROTHER,
WHERE ART THOU?
The Continuum of Sibling Offenses

Cruelty, thy name is sibling. Evil masterminds of torture haven't devised methods as horrific as those conceived by bored twelve-year-olds in suburbia. Here, laid out on a scale of evil of 1 to 100, are just a few examples brotherly and sisterly torment from real live siblings we know.

1
LEAST EVIL

I once took a pancake and shoved it down my brother's throat to shut him up. Now he talks me off the ledge before my mother's visit. —**AMY**

My brother once dragged me by my ankles around my house and gave me severe rug-burn on my back. Now he is a neuro-interventional radiologist and my baby's godfather. —**CARRIE**

EINE KLEINE NACHTEVIL

I rigged a séance. I was twelve and my brother was eight. Tied objects in the room to fishing line. Lights out, candles lit. We pulled the strings and you can guess the rest. Even after I showed him how we rigged it, he was still scared to go to sleep. —**DAVE**

Once my younger sister threw a frozen steak at me, giving me a black eye the day before my eighteenth birthday. —**LAURA**

GETTING SICKER . . .

When I was eighteen, my sister was eight. My parents used to force me to babysit her (without pay, of course). We'd go to the local mall, and I'd tell her to go run up to people and yell, "HEY EVERYBODY, I'M QUEER! HEY EVERYBODY, I'M QUEER!" (Intended in the odd, not gay, sense.) Now

I make her babysit my kid. I pay her, though. And I am never going to let her take him to the mall. —ALEX

....

PRETTY SNEAKY, SIS

My sister used to tell me that my feet smelled like chips (I was obsessed with chips). So almost every day I would bend over and smell my feet and/or lick them. —KATHY

....

When I was fourteen and my sister sixteen she brought her very first boyfriend home to meet the family. As we all sat down to dinner I told her her nose job was healing really nicely.—RITZ

....

EVILER-THAN-THOU

I once threw a teddy bear at my little bother's head because he was being a jerk, and it turned out to be his Teddy Ruxpin (that stupid—and HEAVY—talking bear) and it ended up knocking his two front teeth out. They were his baby teeth, and would have come out sooner or later, but this probably contributed to him having buckteeth for most of his childhood.—JOE

....

We used to tell my youngest brother he was adopted because he doesn't have a birthmark on his stomach like we all did. We even made up an "official" fake birth certificate that "proved" he came from another family (so mean!). —KARA

....

BUDDING-SADISTS ANONYMOUS

When I was six, My three sisters and I played barbers in the bathroom. We got everything we could find in the cupboard and mixed it up in a mug. My sister laid me back on the loo, pasted the mixture all over my face, and shaved it all off with the au pair's razor. She shaved a whole potato peeling of skin off my nose, and it bled for three days. —KITTY

....

100 EVILEST

When I was three, my sister made me drink pee. You see— we took our hygiene very seriously. So . . . when it came to bath time, we set a rule. Before we got in the tub, we had to pee in one of those Halloween plastic pumpkins—as an insurance policy that neither of us peed in the tub. After a few weeks of "collection," she made me drink it.—DANA

FORGIVE OR FORGET?

A Handy Guide

If you were to get into it every single time your sister crossed
the line, you'd spend a good part of your life
in anger-management classes. So learn how to distinguish
between true transgression and minor irritations.

OFFENSE	PICK A FIGHT	LET IT GO
Ruining your H&M dress		X
Ruining your Marni dress	X	
Using you to get to your closet		X
Using you to get to your friends	X	
Killing your goldfish		X
Killing your cat	X	
Blaming something she did on you	X	
Dating someone you hate		X
Marrying someone you hate	X	
Embezzling family funds	X	
Sleeping with a third cousin		X
Sleeping with a first cousin	X	
Sleeping with your ex	X	

ONLY THE LONELY?

Having siblings is no piece of cake, but not having them can be just as hard. Sure, you never had to share your Legos or put up with hand-me-downs, but being an only kid can be lonesome. Still, there's no reason to buy into the hype that only children are poorly adjusted, socially awkward, or otherwise disadvantaged. Just look at this list of impressive sibling-free peeps.

FRANK SINATRA

TIGER WOODS

WILLIAM RANDOLPH HEARST

FDR

JOHN UPDIKE

CARY GRANT

LILLIAN HELLMAN

JOHN LENNON

BOB MARLEY

LEONARDO DA VINCI

CAROL BURNETT

ALBERT EINSTEIN

*Why, exactly, are you forced to gather for holidays,
reunions, and other seemingly random events with these people?
Because they're family. And while your friends may love you,
there's nothing like a blood relative to make you feel connected to the world.*

HOME FOR THE HOLIDAYS

The word "holiday" derives its original meaning from the prefix "holy" (from the middle English *"helig"*), meaning "sacred." Hence, "sacred day." Today, the word has come to mean "vacation" or "day of leisure."

Ironic, no? No words are less likely to spring to mind when we think of the holidays than "sacred," "vacation," or "leisure." And yet, each year, we return to relive the emotional carnage of the family gathering. How to survive? A few helpful tactics:

BUILD IN ALONE TIME. If you're coming home for five days, only tell your parents about three. Spend the first two in a hotel or with an old friend who lives in town so you'll have time to gear up for the visit.

GIVE THE INSANELY STRICT DIET A REST. The sight of a carbohydrate on your plate has been known to elicit screams of terror and haunting visions of fat pants. But pass up Mum's "famous" mashed potatoes, and you're asking for World Wars III and IV all at once. Just eat them.

BUT KEEP SOME SEMBLANCE OF CONTROL. Abandon all restraint and you'll end up hating your family and yourself (even more than usual). Adopt an eating plan, at least for the duration of the stay, which restricts calorie intake but allows flexibility in the types of food you can eat.

DON'T DRINK TOO MUCH. Thought your mum's nagging couldn't possibly sound more irritating? Try listening to it with a hangover. Sure, drinking seems like a good way to ease the pain of the family encounter, but don't overindulge.

DON'T REGRESS. Easier said than done. But just because your brother is acting like a preadolescent brat doesn't mean you have to follow suit. If you find yourself using phrases like "Up your nose with a rubber hose" and/or "Fuck you, Grandma," give yourself a time-out.

DON'T USE THE HOLIDAYS AS A PLATFORM TO DENOUNCE YOUR PARENTS' FAITH. Yes, you may take issue with certain passages in the Bible. You may object to your family's beliefs. You may even have recently pledged your soul to Satan. Good for you. It's a free country, but that doesn't mean you have to pick a fight with your kinsmen on the very day they're trying to celebrate their faith.

BREAK OUT THE SCRABBLE. Conversation is overrated. Sure, it starts off pleasantly enough. But before you know it, Dad and Uncle Joel are arm wrestling near the china and Grandpa's talking trash about Mum's stuffing. Games keep everyone occupied without mining the more dangerous psyches of the players. Everyone laughs, competitive urges are channeled, and the time passes without incident.

• •

TODAY, THE MODERN FAMILY has scattered to the four corners of the globe. Most of us leave home after school; parents get divorced; even once-close siblings lose touch. But while it may take a bit more effort to maintain ties, it's usually worth it. They're the only family you have. And it may at times be hard to love your brother while he's picking his nose and trying to make you eat it, but do your best. Didn't your dad tell you that was all he expected of you?

is for
LUXURY

lux • u • ry \'lək-sh(ə)rē\ *n.* **1.** Something conducive to pleasure and comfort. *(You don't know* luxury *until you've had a two-hour hot-stone massage.)* **2.** Sumptuous surroundings, as well as that which contributes to such an environment. **3.** A thing whose value is determined by anything other than need.

YOU GRAB YOUR COFFEE, TURN ON YOUR COMPUTER,

and there it is. The headline's almost as big as the screen: "Random Celebrity Buys Fabulous Caribbean Island. Secretly Clones Sir John Gielgud to Create Race of Superbutlers to Mix Fruity Drinks."

A mix of emotions floods your system. Disgust at our culture of excess. Wonder at the sheer scale of such obnoxious consumption. And, in spite of yourself, rabid envy of the lifestyle of the privileged elite. Finally, remorse for your own materialistic desires.

Now, now. Contrary to popular belief, enjoying luxe things is not a sin. As long as you keep it in perspective and find luxury in the small things. Be it a special-edition pen set or your very own Lear jet, the trick is to find your own way of living well—within your means. (Okay, with the occasional foray into irresponsible extravagance.) Luxury isn't about overspending or ostentatious consumption: It's about enjoying life.

*Some things are undeniably luxurious. They may not be within everyone's reach,
but they give us something to aspire to (or not).*

LUXURY vs. GAUDY
A Handy Chart

Money can buy lots of things. But living large is not the same as living
well. So how can you tell the cream of the crop from the bottom of the
barrel? Train your eye and fake it until then. Here's a quick guide to get
you started:

LUXURIOUS	GAUDY
600-THREAD-COUNT EGYPTIAN COTTON SHEETS	SATIN SHEETS
MONOGRAMMED CASHMERE SLIPPERS	MONOGRAMMED CAR
DRINKING CHAMPAGNE	BATHING IN CHAMPAGNE
CASHMERE ROBE	FUR ROBE
HEN PARTY AT WYNN LAS VEGAS	WEDDING AT WYNN LAS VEGAS
VOSGES CHOCOLATES	CHOCOLATE BODY PAINT
CADILLAC	HUMMER
PENTHOUSE SUITE	PLAYBOY MANSION
SPEAKING TWO FOREIGN LANGUAGES	HAVING SEX WITH TWO FOREIGNERS AT A TIME

*Big rocks and fast cars have their appeal. But luxury doesn't have to mean
breaking the bank. From going faux to relishing the small things
to mixing the occasional high-end purchase with your own playful style,
luxury's all about living well outside the (Tiffany) box.*

BUT IS IT WORTH IT?

Hard to say. One woman's splurge is another woman's insanity.
That's why if you're Betsy, £400 jeans are a quality investment that
quickly pay for themselves through multiple uses and good-arse self-
esteem, but if you're Melina, a pair of Levi's will fit the bill—without
the bill. That said, these guidelines will pretty much ensure a guilt-
free expenditure:

IT'S A KEEPER. THINK ARTWORK, HANDBAGS, CLASSIC SHOES,
PORCELAIN TEACUPS, A COUNTRY HOUSE.

IT MARKS A SPECIAL OCCASION. THIS INCLUDES YOUR
GOT-A-RAISE BRACELET AND YOUR NEW BIRKIN.

IT INVOLVES GETTING ON A PLANE. NO ONE EVER
REGRETS VACATIONS, ESPECIALLY TO PLACES THEY'VE NEVER BEEN.

IT'S QUIRKY AND VERY YOU. LET EVERYONE ELSE SPEND
THEIR BENJAMINS BUYING THE SAME FROCK
EVERYONE ELSE IS WEARING. YOU SHOULD SPEND IT ON BUILDING
YOUR VINTAGE COCKTAIL-SHAKER COLLECTION.

When to Fake It

Ours is a world of knockoffs and shabby substitutes.
And hooray for that. Because sometimes, faux is the way to go.

REAL THING	SUBSITUTE	WHEN TO FAKE IT	WHY
FUR	FAUX FUR	ALWAYS	Sure, it's soft. Sure, it's fuzzy. Trouble is, it's an animal with those same attributes. Plus, faux fur comes in bright pink. Minks and seals don't.
PERFUME	DESIGNER IMPOSTER	NEVER	One word: Stench.
MOISTURIZER	CHEAPER VERSIONS	SOMETIMES	For your body, most any will do. For your face and neck, better to pay for what works for you.
DIAMONDS	CUBIC ZIRC	SOMETIMES	Sparkly earrings? No one will know the difference.
DESIGNER BAGS	KNOCKOFFS	RARELY	A great forgery is a thing of beauty. But your pleasure may be marred by the knowledge that it's a fake. And how genuine do you think that £15 LV wallet really looks?
LINGERIE	TRASHY LINGERIE	OFTEN	La Perla looks great to you, but he can't tell the difference from Frederick's of Hollywood. (In fact, many guys prefer trashy over lacy and pricey.) If you want to splurge, do it for yourself, not for him— and make sure it's comfy.
WINE	PLONK	OFTEN	Nothing sets the mood like a chilled bottle of Cristal. But a quality liquor store will sell many excellent vintages and sparkling wines for about £15.

CHEAP SPLURGES

Toasted baguette sliced in half + butter+ raspberry jam transforms breakfast from bread and butter to a *tartine.*

Set the table with a tablecloth and nice napkins.

Drink Slush Puppies.

Eat a frozen Snickers. Sliced.

Wear something that no one can see: a tattoo, blue panties, a belly chain (so tacky when visible).

Discover the beauty of Dunkin' Donuts coffee.

Have a secret.

Keep the secret. From everyone.

HIGHS AND LOWS
A GUIDE TO MIXING IT UP

To have some fun with the concept of luxury, consider injecting it into unusual contexts:

1. Reupholster the interior of your old VW Golf with Hermès fabric.

2. Wear diamond earrings with your most trashed Levi's.

3. Wear cashmere socks with your Converse trainers.

4. Skip fancy breeders and adopt a rescue pup from the shelter (always).

5. Pick one great pair of shoes per season and build your look around them. A good pair of boots can make any outfit.

6. Do mundane tasks by candlelight. Whether for a quiet dinner at home or at bathtime, candles cast a dreamy glow on even the most modest surroundings.

A THING
OF BEAUTY IS A JOY FOREVER.

Or at least that's how it feels when you're staring at a £3,000 cashmere coat in the window of Harvey Nichols. Life is made just a bit more fun by the occasional splurge and once-in-a-while extravagance. But (oh, you knew there was a "but") as wonderful and exciting as owning something pretty can be, it would be a shame to allow luxury to be defined only by the things you can buy. Sometimes, just sitting in the park on a sunny day, latte in hand, can be the most luxurious, indulgent thing in the world. And lying in bed all day with the Sunday paper in one hand and the remote in the other? We wouldn't trade it for all the swank black-tie events in the world.

is for
MONEY

mon • ey \\'mə-nē\ *n.*
1. Cash, or other such
tender used to purchase
goods, services, and one-
way tickets to Tahiti. **2.**
The root of all evil. **3.** A source of great pleasure and great stress. (*A fool and his* money
*are soon parted, but the fool probably has fun
along the way.*).

IF YOU DON'T HAVE ANY, YOU WANT SOME.

If you have some, you want more. And if you have more, you're probably living in perpetual fear that people are using you to get at it.

Any way you look at it, money is a loaded issue.

In our tell-all society, affairs with great-nieces and schoolteachers are hardly the stuff of scandal anymore. Celebutantes tell Oprah all about their lifelong battle with depression. We admit to the strangers next to us in AA the sloppy details of our powerlessness when faced with a fifth of Jack Daniel's. But we still pause before telling our best friend how much take-home pay we see every two weeks. And we're afraid to ask our boss for an (objectively) much-deserved raise.

Why? Probably because we fall into the trap of equating money with value. Big mistake. The former is a question of economics. The latter is a function of all-around goodness, and other highly subjective intangibles. Don't feel bad, we all do that thing where we wonder whether our lawyer friend Scotty isn't somehow ultimately better off because he is charging £400/hour. And he's doing so legally.

Which brings us to the other faulty fiscal assumption: Equating money with happiness. True, money can buy plane tickets and nice shoes and great bottles of Brunello di Montalcino. But it can't put an uncontrollable spring in your step or a smile on your face. (Okay, maybe it can. But once you've figured out how to channel the joy without jiggling the coin, you're in a better place.)

People spend a lot of time thinking about money.
They should consider how to enjoy it.

MAKING MONEY

Dire Straits sang of getting "your money for nothing and your chicks for free." Nice work if you can get it, but the rest of us have to follow the Donna Summer route and "work hard for the money." Or not. There are almost as many ways to get it as there are ways to spend it.

INHERIT IT *The Easy Way*

PROS:	You never worry where the next rent check is coming from. Multiple summer houses. Great boarding school stories. Strong liver, stronger tolerance for gin.
CONS:	Trusts broken, lawsuits. Occasional sense of uselessness and guilt.
SPENDING PROFILE:	"This round's on me."

MARRY IT *The Lame Way*

PROS:	Private jets. Diamonds on demand. Lots of vacation homes. Closets full of pretty designer dresses.
CONS:	The next trophy wife looms around every bend.
SPENDING PROFILE:	Amex Centurion.

EARN IT *The Most Common Way*

PROS:	Guilt-free income. A job well done. Inimitable inner glow that comes from knowledge that you got there on your own.
CONS:	1/16 share in summer house.
SPENDING PROFILE:	Dutch.

Dropping cash is easy.
Budgeting—and still having as much fun—is harder.

Budgeting for Dummies

KEEP A MONEY DIARY FOR TWO WEEKS. RECORD EVERYTHING YOU SPEND. IT WILL BE EASY TO FIGURE OUT WHERE YOU'RE WASTING. BEFORE YOU BUY IT, ASK YOURSELF IF YOU REALLY NEED/WANT IT. THE NEXT TIME YOU GO SHOPPING, TRY THIS EXERCISE: FOR EVERY NEW THING THAT YOU BRING INTO YOUR HOME, YOU HAVE TO REMOVE SOMETHING ELSE IN ITS PLACE. (YOU MIGHT FIND THAT YOU'RE HAPPY WITH THE JEANS AND IPOD YOU ALREADY OWN.) CONSOLIDATE: USE ONE CREDIT CARD. GET A CABLE/INTERNET/DIGITAL PHONE PLAN. EARMARK SOME OF YOUR SALARY AS SAVINGS. SET IT UP THROUGH DIRECT DEPOSIT. (YOU'LL NEVER REMEMBER TO TRANSFER A BIT EVERY MONTH.) IF SOMEONE WANTS TO GIVE YOU SOMETHING FOR NOTHING, THERE IS ALWAYS A CATCH. THERE IS NO SUCH THING AS GETTING FOURTEEN CDS FOR £1. TRY NOT TO CARRY DEBT. THE INTEREST WILL KILL YOU.

The key with money—as with romance, food, work, and family—is to be aware of what you're doing with what you have. The worst thing about money is feeling as if you have no control over it. Try not to fall into that sort of negative thinking. You do have control. You've earned it, after all. Now just do what you want to do with it.

is for
NEVER

nev • er \'ne-vər\ *n*. Not ever; on no occasion; at no time. *(It's over. I am never calling that loser again.)*

"NEVER SAY 'NEVER.'"

People like to say that. They also like to say "Nothing's impossible" and "You never know until you try." Why? Beats us. Sometimes you do (or should) know before you try. Some things really are impossible. And sometimes, just sometimes, you should say 'never.'

Growing up, becoming your own person, self realization: Yes, they require reaching your potential, pushing the envelope, and exceeding expectations. But they also entail setting boundaries, rising above the bullshit, and not wasting your time on lame people and dull activities. And it's this second category we're concerned with in this chapter. No fancy quizzes or complicated instructions, just a quick-reading, no-fooling list of things not to do. Ever. Seriously.

NEVER round up when guessing someone's age. **NEVER** allow your friends to drink and dial. **NEVER** challenge the accuracy of your fuel gauge. E means E. There is no such thing as E-ish. **NEVER** be afraid to make your own gifts. **NEVER** shoplift. **NEVER** wear stilettos to a football match. **NEVER** forget your passport when traveling to foreign countries. **NEVER** open your parents' door without asking. **NEVER** open your grandparents' door without asking. **NEVER** stop yourself from saying something nice. **NEVER** refuse a compliment. **NEVER** fake an orgasm. (You ruin it for all the women who don't.) **NEVER** pass gas and forget to blame it on the dog (if available). **NEVER** deny yourself the last bite of something really delicious. **NEVER** miss the chance to enjoy a guilty pleasure. (The guilt never seems to last very long.) **NEVER** let old folks struggle with a door. **NEVER** assume someone with dreadlocks is a Rastafarian. **NEVER** neglect any areas of a scratch-off lottery ticket. **NEVER** feel bad about cheating during a workout. **NEVER** go to bed angry. Get it out beforehand, because otherwise you'll just lay there stewing. **NEVER** make mean/bored/unhappy faces at a wedding. There's a good chance you're being filmed or photographed. **NEVER** use obscenities or make rude hand gestures in Bahrain, United Arab Emirates, or Kenya. **NEVER** sunbathe nude in India. **NEVER** chew gum in Singapore. **NEVER** import pork to Yemen (it's a crime punishable by death). **NEVER** eat cheap blowfish. **NEVER** sing in a public Floridian place while wearing a swimsuit. **NEVER** make fun of somebody's smile. Teeth are fair game. **NEVER** be the one to break the news regarding Santa Claus, the Tooth Fairy, or any other personas with good reputations. **NEVER** go against your gut. **NEVER** hit and run. **NEVER** decline a high five. **NEVER** pass up a homemade baked good (unless it's being offered to you by a sworn enemy). **NEVER** exit a restroom without washing your hands. **NEVER** cheat unless you're playing with known cheaters (because in that case you're just playing by the rules). **NEVER** kick a kitty or pup. **NEVER** trash recyclables.

NEVER say, "This stinks," and then make someone smell it. NEVER spill the beans. NEVER take your health for granted. NEVER feel inclined to tell the truth to total strangers. NEVER get off the phone with a telemarketer without telling them to remove your name from their call list. NEVER exclude "I have no idea" as a response if it's the truth. NEVER take credit for something you didn't do. NEVER throw nonbiodegradable objects out the window. NEVER hold on to old socks for sentimental reasons. NEVER accept a package from a stranger at the airport. NEVER use chopsticks to pass food to another person's chopsticks, plate, or bowl when eating in a Japanese restaurant. NEVER pick your teeth at the table. NEVER buy a used mattress. NEVER trust a salesperson's judgment. *Of course they think it looks good on you.* NEVER be afraid to send a man flowers. NEVER procrastinate with the fun stuff. NEVER lie about having an STD.

There. Now that you're in touch with the affirmative power of the occasional blanket negative, we can move on.

is for
OFFSPRING

 **off • spring** \'of-spring\ *n.* **1.** Progeny considered as a group. **2.** A child of particular parentage. **3.** The typical result of a pregnancy or adoption.

YOUR LIFE

can be neatly divided into five fifteen-year phases, each of which entails being controlled by a different set of tyrants. For the first fifteen, it's your parents. Then you graduate to a therapist, who charges you for the privilege of bossing you around. Phase three: the one where everyone and her mother tells you how to raise your kids. Next, when your kids turn fifteen, all the baggage from the first three phases will come home to roost as your children become your new masters, staying out all night, talking back, and making you beg your GP for Prozac. Finally, at the end, you will be ordered about by a cadre of people so depressing—cruise directors, podiatrists, politicians—that you will welcome death with open arms.

But we digress. Because it is the middle period to which this chapter is devoted. Having babies is both the greatest miracle of your life and the occasion on which a procession of soothsayers, witch doctors, and snake-oil peddlers find it perfectly appropriate to assault you with an endless onslaught of know-it-all-ism.

So we're not even going to get into dictating what right and wrong parenting is. Because there are as many parenting methods out there as there are parents, and only a few of them yield children who grow up to be Charles Manson (or worse, Paris Hilton). What we will do: give you our two cents and some basic knowledge. Plus some advice on what to do with that extra nappy-rash cream.

Well, you've gone and gotten yourself knocked up.
That was the easy part.

CH-CH-CH-CH-
CHANGES
Bidding Adieu to Size Tens, Restful Nights, and a Few Friends

Up to this point, the concept of "adjusting" meant futzing with the antenna on your radio to get better reception and "weight gain" meant ten pounds here and there. Hear that? It's the sound of God laughing at you. A rundown of the changes to come:

1. **YOUR BODY.** Sure, maternity clothes are cuter than they used to be. And yes, those prenatal yoga classes can keep you in relatively good shape. But one truth is unavoidable: You will get huge. It's just what happens.

How *much* weight you gain is entirely between you and your doc (we know one woman who, while pregnant with twins, gained so much she considered naming them Ben and Jerry). But now might be a good time to shelve your impossible standards of attractiveness. Pregnant women are totally beautiful.

2. **YOUR SEX LIFE.** Imagine, for a moment, that you got hit by a truck. Not a big truck, mind you. Let's say a midsize SUV. That's what a delivery is like for most women.

Now add to that the effect of painkillers, a mercurial digestive tract, and sleep deprivation. If you're in the first few weeks of breast-feeding, you might have a fever and a lot of soreness. Oh, and your once-swollen belly now looks like a deflated balloon.

These are just the kind of passion-inducing aphrodisiacs that kick off parenthood. Is it any wonder that you're not the sex tiger you once were? For some, a healthy sex life returns after about two months. For others, it just never quite revs back up to what it was before. (A good number of doctors tell mums at their six-week follow-up visit—at which point most get the go-ahead to start getting busy again—that if they'd rather their take-home orders be "no sex for another six weeks," they'll back them up.)

3. YOUR SOCIAL LIFE. Something happens to people when they have kids; namely, they tend to disappear off the face of the earth. Suddenly, your childless friends don't seem to understand you anymore. You envy their freedom and fret that they now regard you as a boring geezer. So you tell yourself that all of their pursuits are selfish, and that they have no idea what it's like to care for someone, and you're better off without them and any of the fun they claim to have.

As usual, the truth lies somewhere between the extremes, so we recommend you try to resist this kind of black-and-white thinking. You may end up losing a few pals who can't wrap their brains around the fact that you're not out doing lines of coke off their naked bodies. But odds are they were probably not the friends for you. As for everyone else, well, not only will they understand, they'll become part of your invaluable support network if you continue to make time for them.

4. YOUR SCHEDULE. Whoever coined the phrase "sleep like a baby" clearly did not have one. Babies do not sleep like babies; they sleep like college students—sporadically and unpredictably. In fact, early child-rearing was made for insomniacs.

But the good news is this: It doesn't last long. Most babies start sleeping through the night (by which the experts mean midnight to five a.m.) at around three months. Before you know it, years will fly by and they'll be leaving you behind for the night.

MOTHERHOOD + PAPARAZZI=
FUN FOR THE WHOLE COUNTRY

Connect the celebrity mum to the concept most associated with her progeny.

MUM	CONCEPT
1. Gwyneth Paltrow	**A.** International relations
2. The three Kates *(Well, two Kates and a Cate—Winslet, Moss, and Blanchett)*	**B.** Nude Awakening
	C. Pseudo-British composure
3. Madonna	**D.** British composure
4. Angelina Jolie	
5. Catherine Zeta-Jones	**E.** Keeping the doctor away
6. Demi Moore	**F.** Geriatric dad

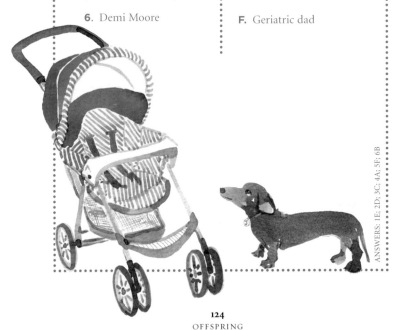

ANSWERS: 1E; 2D; 3C; 4A; 5F; 6B

STOP THE MADNESS
How to Do a Better Job Than Your Parents

Remember when we told you we weren't going to tell you what to do? We lied. There are a few things you just shouldn't do, and chances are your parents (or at least one of your friends' parents) did it. And if you want a chance to stop the snowball effect in its nasty tracks, just be sure to refrain from:

1. **PUTTING BABIES ON THEIR STOMACHS TO SLEEP.** Doctors say that can be one of the causes of the dreaded Sudden Infant Death Syndrome (SIDS).

2. **GIVING KIDS APPLE JUICE BEFORE BED.** Bad for teeth, say dentists. Full of sugar, say doctors. Smells bad, says us.

3. **SHAKING YOUR KID.** Um, duh.

4. **PLAYING FAVORITES.** It's just rude. Prove to a child that there's enough love to go around, and you'll do wonders for his self-esteem and confidence. (Bonus: Experts say he'll also tend to misbehave less, since he isn't constantly yearning for attention.)

5. **OVERPROTECTING.** From the Bible to *The Catcher in the Rye,* the annals of literary history are filled with laments over the loss of innocence. But, well, sometimes the world really does suck, and unless you hermetically seal your children in an Edenlike biodome, they're probably going to find out about it. The best you can do? Prepare them—and yourself.

6. **MARTYRING YOURSELF BY HAVING NO LIFE OUTSIDE OF YOUR KIDS.** Working and stay-at-home parents alike, listen up: Denying yourself any activity outside the home and office leads to self-pity, boredom, and a general pattern of passive-aggressive behavior. (For more on this, see The Mother Translator in "K is for Kin.")

BUTT FACE:

A & D Ointment for Your Face

Rock-a-bye baby,
asleep on my lap.
Since you were born,
my skin looks
like crap.

Child-care duties forcing you to neglect your complexion? Bring back a healthy glow with a secret weapon sitting right on your changing table: A & D Nappy Rash Cream.

Yes, really. Sometimes salvation comes in the most unlikely forms. Cortisone may fight flakiness. All those prettily packaged hopes-in-a-jar may smell great. But there's a tiny miracle in A&D's magical blend of zinc oxide and aloe. And it costs a mere four quid.

One smear and your skin will be as soft and flawless as— sorry, but we couldn't resist— your baby's bottom.

SWAP TILL YOU DROP
Getting Something for Nothing

Kids. Love 'em. Except for one thing: They grow. Just when you've fallen in love with the £50 booties, the cashmere cable-knit sweater, and the suede onesie, he gains three pounds.

Why invest all that cash in new loot? He won't appreciate it. (Not the way you would appreciate, say, a postpartum leather miniskirt.) Host a swap instead. It's easy.

1. Invite eight to ten mums whose kids are more or less the same age.

2. Everyone brings new or gently used items in the following categories: clothing (no puke stains, please), toys (with all working parts), books, videos, CDs, carrying contraptions, sleepwear, and other paraphernalia. (Feeding devices must be unused.) Unwanted presents, stuff that bores them, stuff that bores you—all someone else's treasure.

3. Break out the vino and start shopping.

4. ROUND ONE: Everyone gets to pick their two favorite things.

5. ROUND TWO: Free for all. (Let's remember to be civilized. This is not a sample sale.)

6. Box any leftovers for delivery to a local women's shelter.

WE'D BE LIARS

if we pretended we knew the magic formula for perfect parenting. Or if we pretended anyone did, for that matter. But of course, we press on, fueled by the optimistic belief that it's possible to raise smart, ethical beings. If they have a sense of humor and taste in clothes, well, that's just icing on the cake.

is for

PARTY

par · ty \ˈpär-tē\ **1.** *n.* A social gathering designed for pleasure or amusement. **2.** *v.* To celebrate or carouse at, or as if at, a party. *(Did someone forget to go home after that* party *last night?)* **3.** See also: bash, blowout, bacchanal, fête, gala, and scene.

AT ITS BEST,

a party is no mere congregation of friends around a freshly tapped keg (although there's nothing wrong with that); it's an event that takes on a memorable life of its own. No matter what the occasion, from a Tuesday potluck to a lost weekend in Vegas, there are two ways to do parties: You're either having a party or going to one. Here's a look at both.

An at-home party is intimate and charming, but it's a heck of a lot of work.
Herewith, a few tips and tricks to streamline the process.

RSVP CHEZ MOI

Oh, it's not so hard. Just think: time line and to-do list.

UPON DECLARING YOU'RE HAVING A PARTY

____ Figure out what kind of party you're having.

____ Draw up the guest list.

____ Decide on food and drinks.

____ Arrange to rent, buy, or borrow whatever you might need, i.e. tables, chairs, helium tanks, margarita fountain.

____ Send invitations.

ONE WEEK AHEAD

____ Do a major house-cleaning.

____ Make a grocery list.

____ Place special orders: catering, cakes, flowers, massive quantities of anything.

FOUR DAYS AHEAD

____ Check RSVPs, call anyone who needs to be called.

____ Do bulk shopping.

____ Make mixes and load into iPod or burn CDs.

TWO DAYS

____ Prepare food that can be stored.

____ Clean or have the house cleaned.

ONE DAY

____ Pick up anything you're borrowing or renting.

____ Shop for perishables.

____ Set up tables, chairs, sound system, any seating areas.

____ Store any fragile or, er, personal items you don't want to subject to the party.

DAY OF

____ Prepare the rest of the food.

____ Set up the bar (remember lemon and lime wedges).

____ Set the tables or arrange the area you've allotted for food.

____ Put flowers and candles in their places.

____ Set up garbage and recycling receptacles.

THREE HOURS

____ Add finishing touches.

____ Set out cheese or bowls of nonperishable snacks.

ONE HOUR

____ Get dressed.

T MINUS 30 MINUTES

____ Open wine.

____ Put perishable snacks in their places.

____ Turn on music.

No, you don't have to slave all day in the kitchen. Unless, of course, you want to.

WHAT A FRIEND
WE HAVE IN CHEESES
Composing the Perfect Cheese Board

Can't deal with cooking? It doesn't take more than cheese to make a party. Note: The Cheese Board should not be confused with the Cheese Plate. One is elegant, the other passé. One will score you big party points, the other will simply encourage the eating of cheese. (Which, of course, is not entirely a bad thing.)

TIER ONE: THE BASICS
Readily available at the supermarket, won't cost an arm and a leg, a good starter kit

BRIE

SMOKED GOUDA

MILD DANISH BLUE CHEESE

GOAT CHEESE

TIER TWO: THE INTERNATIONAL BASICS
The first step into the larger world of more complicated flavors

FRENCH: **CAMEMBERT** and **MORBIER**—distinct flavors that add depth

SPANISH: the ever-popular **MANCHEGO** and a crumbly **CABRALES**

ITALIAN: **BOCCONCINI** and **GORGONZOLA** soften things up

TIER THREE: HEAVY HITTERS
Rarely seen inside grocer's dairy aisle, may cost an arm and a leg (as well as a spleen)

TALEGGIO: brilliant stinky Italian

VACHERIN DU MONT D'OR: scoopy French

MONTENEBRO: soft Spanish goat

DETAILS, DETAILS, DETAILS:

Assemble cheeses on wood board.

Each cheese should have its own knife.

Accessorize with carbs (crackers, good bread, mini toasts)
and sweets (grapes, figs, dried cranberries, dates, chutneys, honey).

CYOB

Creating Your Own Beverage

Expecting a crowd but don't want to stock a full bar? Go for a theme drink. How will you come up with a soon-to-be-legendary InsertNameHere-tini? Easy.

1. Favorite color + natural disaster

   "PINK HURRICANE"

   "BLUE AVALANCHE"

   "GREEN TWISTER"

2. Exotic locale + any word you might see featured in a comic book fight that starts with the same letter

   "BAJA BLAST"

   "BELIZE BLAMMO!"

   "KANSAS CITY KAZAAM!"

   "PEORIA POW!"

3. Your pet's name + "-tini," "-nog," or "-politan"

   "BREWSTERPOLITAN"

   "ABBYTINI"

   "DOGNOG"

4. Sexual practice + land formation

   "FOREPLAY ON THE MOUNTAIN"

   "MAKEOUT ON THE MESA"

   "69 ON THE STATE LINE"

Okay. Maybe not that last one.

HERE'S MUD IN YOUR EYE
Giving the Perfect Toast

Be sincere and max out at three to five minutes. Tell a cute story, but leave out the raunchy escapades, unless it's a hen party. Even then, consider the company—as well as the elderly couple at the next table—before screaming out, "But that was *nothing* compared to the gang bang of '98!" Finish things off with a culturally appropriate exclamation from the chart below:

CHINESE
WEN LIE!

IRISH
SLAINTE!

ITALIAN
SALUTE!

FRENCH
À VOTRE SANTÉ!

JAPANESE
KAMPAI!

GERMAN
PROSIT!

POLISH
NA ZDROWIE!

GREEK
YASAS!

RUSSIAN
ZA VASHE ZDOROVYE!

HEBREW
L'CHAIM!

SPANISH
SALUD!

MAORI
KIA ORA!

HUNGARIAN
EGE SZE GE RE!

SWEDISH
SKAL!

Whether you're attending a wedding on the Riviera or your neighbor's backyard BBQ, being a stellar guest will not only ensure your invite the next time around, but will guarantee you have a good time.

THE
TEN COMMANDMENTS
OF BEING
A GOOD GUEST

I

THOU SHALT GREET YOUR HOSTS AS SOON AS YOU ARRIVE.

(This is especially important if you don't know them well.)

**THOU SHALT SAY GOOD-BYE
AND THANK YOU BEFORE YOU LEAVE.**

II

THOU SHALT BE RESPECTFUL OF OTHERS' HOMES.

*(This means use coasters, no feet on the couch, and if you spill, clean it up.
If the spill is really bad, offer to pay the cleaning bill.)*

III

**THOU SHALT PLACE ALL RUBBISH IN
APPROPRIATE RECEPTACLES.**

IV

THOU SHALT 'FESS UP IF YOU BREAK SOMETHING.

*(Especially if you stop up a toilet. Should you discover someone else's jam,
thou shalt tell the host ASAP and proclaim your innocence.)*

V

**THOU SHALT, WHEN AT A SEATED DINNER, WAIT FOR THE
HOST AND/OR HOSTESS TO TAKE THE FIRST BITE.**

VI

WHEN INSIDE, THOU SHALT USE INSIDE VOICES.

VII

THOU SHALT ALWAYS MAKE EYE CONTACT WHILE TOASTING.

VIII

THOU SHALT KEEP THY PDA TO A MINIMUM.

(Unless you're at a swingers party.)

IX

THOU SHALT OFFER TO HELP.

(Your host will probably decline, but it's the thought that counts.)

X

THOU SHALT NOT OVERSTAY YOUR WELCOME.

THAT WAS SO MUCH FUN!

The Art of the Thank-You Note

Everyone appreciates them as much as you do, so make them a habit. Don't know what to say? This handy formula works like a charm.

1. GREETING + NAME.
    Example: Dear Patty, *Or:* Hi, Russell

2. EXPRESSION OF GRATITUDE followed by a reference to the reason you're writing.
    Example: Thank you so much for the lovely party.
    Or: Thank you so much for your hospitality.

3. INCLUDE A HIGHLIGHT.
    Example: Your meatloaf was delicious!
    Or: The DJ was fantastic. I haven't danced like that in a long time.

4. LOOK AT THE BIG PICTURE.
    Example: It was great to hang out. Let's get together again soon.
    Or: I'm so glad we had the chance to see one another.
    Hope to see you again soon.

5. CLOSING STATEMENT.
    Example: Thanks again.
    Or: Not to lay it on too thick, but thanks again.

6. SIGNING OFF.
    Example: Love *Or:* All the best *Or:* Yours truly

Now you know how to have a party and how to go to a party. Really, there's no mystery to it once you figure out how you like to have fun. So let's move on to life's other quandaries.

is for
QUANDARIES

quan • da • ries \'kwän-d(ə)rēz\
n. **1.** A state of confusion or uncertainty **2.** A dilemma that may be accompanied by unwelcome dermatological side effects, including brow wrinkles and stress-induced acne *(I have a total quandary-induced breakout)* **3.** Questions best answered by self-proclaimed mavens and know-it-alls.

YOU'VE GOT
QUESTIONS?
DAILYCANDY'S GOT ANSWERS.

Three plus five? Eight. Capital of Minnesota? Saint to the Paul. What do you do when your friend borrows your cashmere sweater and returns it with a Syrah stain twice the size of the Australian Outback? See, now, technically, that one's more of a quandary. When you find yourself in a pickle with not one issue to consider, but many, the answers get more complicated, and amazingly entertaining.

On Friendship

Dear DailyCandy,
Whenever the check comes, my friend Fran either makes a run for the ladies' room, comes up short, or says she'll get it next time. I'm tired of covering her cocktails—and so is everyone else. How can I talk to her about this?   SINCERELY, GOING FOR BROKE

Dear Broke,
Sounds like Fran is one "Oops, I forgot my wallet" away from being a full-on grifter. Tell her you've noticed she hasn't been putting in her fair share and you weren't sure if it was money troubles or just an oversight. Tell her that you're happy to frequent cheaper joints or eat in. If she doesn't pull her weight after that, you're officially allowed to never dine with her again. What are you, made of money?

Dear DailyCandy,
I've double-booked myself on Saturday night. Again. It happens every weekend: I commit to multiple things and by the time they come around, I forget or just don't feel like doing them. What to do?
                                SINCERELY, TWO-TIMING IN TAUNTON

Dear Two-Timing,
Generally speaking, honor the first commitment. It's bad form to cancel just because something more enticing comes along. That said, the occasional last-minute bail is generally acceptable. Example: If you have plans with your best friend and your crush suddenly asks you out, if she's a true friend she'll not only understand, she'll even help you figure out what to wear.

On Dating

Dear DailyCandy,

Me and my boyfriend? Totally in love. Me and my boyfriend's friends? Let's just say we make the Cold War seem like a warm breeze. They've been friends since kindergarten, now they're totally different—my boyfriend is a mature adult, and they are numbskulls who can't stop with the fart jokes. How can I let it be known that I'd rather never hang out with them ever again?

SINCERELY, BALL AND CHAIN IN BALHAM

Dear Ball and Chain,

Here's news for you: There's a 99 percent chance your boyfriend makes fart jokes when you're not around. Maybe he makes them in his head when you're around.

This being what it is, he and his friends might not have anything else in common except for that they've spent most of their lives together. They share a love of Coach Rudy, and all had crushes on Molly McAfee. The past is totally major. Try to appreciate that they've stuck it out all these years. This may even endear you to them. It doesn't have to be a lovefest, but refrain from rolling your eyes when one of them says something stupid, and they may like you enough to keep the peace. And if you make a fart joke, they'll fall at your feet.

Dear DailyCandy,

About three weeks ago, I received an e-mail from a friend of a friend who'd spotted me at a party. I didn't remember him, but he was funny and charming. It quickly grew into an e-mail flirtation. After three weeks of back and forth, we decided to meet. A total bust! He was awkward, chewed with his mouth open, and wasn't the least bit funny. On my way home I swore I'd never talk to him again, but this morning he sent another e-mail. Should I respond?

SINCERELY, REAR-ENDED ON THE INFORMATION SUPERHIGHWAY

Dear Rear-Ended,

What a modern quandary you have. But let's rephrase the question. Should you pursue a relationship with someone who you have no chemistry with? Put like that, the answer is pretty obviously "nope." When a guy's only good over text or e-mail, there's a chance that it's not even him at all. You could be falling for the work of a team of dudes on the other side of the computer screen. Plus, even if he gives great Internet, can you take an e-mail to the movies? No. Can an e-mail make you breakfast? Nope. Can you snuggle up with an e-mail?

Dear DailyCandy,
Missy and Clive went out for two years-ish. They broke up six weeks ago (it was mutual). Clive called last night to ask me out. Missy and I are friendly, but I wouldn't say friends. She's my flatmate's friend's friend. I like Clive, but the last thing I want to be is a ghag (Girl-Hating Girl). So, do tell, when exactly does the moratorium lift? It does lift, right?

SINCERELY, SLOPPY SECONDS IN SLOUGH

Dear Sloppy,
Let's just say right off the bat, if you care about your friendship with your friend, the answer is never. No matter what she may say—"Oh I'm fine with it," "I'm totally over him," "I couldn't care less" —don't listen, because that's just lip service. She is not and never will be okay with it, even after she's married. So just don't do it if you care about the friend. If you don't care about the friend, then go for it.

Dear DailyCandy,
Mitch and I have worked together for the past two years. We have great chem, but we're both totally pro when it comes to our jobs. As a general rule, I know office romance is a no-no, but why? Is there a way to pull it off?

SINCERELY, HARDLY WORKING IN WINCHESTER

Dear Hardly,
No diggity, no doubt, there are cons to dating in the workplace. First off, you'll be bringing your personal life to work and vice versa. Then consider that you'll be spending double time together; if you break up you still have to spend five days a week with your ex, and in general people are nosy and they'll be all up in your beeswax and talk behind your backs. However. There are sensible ways to go about it. Set boundaries from the beginning. Keep PDA to a minimum, and don't discuss your personal life at the office.

On Daily Life

Dear DailyCandy,

What do you think is lamer? Being out at some bar and seeing your neighbor's boyfriend sipping pink drinks with some scantily clad chica or having the door slammed in your face the next day when trying to tell said friend? Though I've experienced both, I'm torn. They both pretty much sucked. What do you think?

SINCERELY, DUTY-BOUND IN DUNDEE

Dear Duty,

Yeah, about that. Well. They both suck. In order to avoid being shot as the messenger, you mustn't become the messenger. Unless it's a close friend talk to the cheater before bringing it up to give him the opportunity to come clean.

You don't want to get in the middle of someone else's relationship. It gets very messy and can be way worse than watching someone enjoy a cosmo or having a faceplant come to you.

Dear DailyCandy,

I've always played by the rules. I've never miscounted during Sorry!, peeked at my neighbour's cards during poker, or even used any of my coworkers' secrets against them to get ahead. Yet I, a straightforward, hard-working, loyal, noble individual, sit here at the bottom of the social, professional, and economic totem pole while dishonest, manipulative souls get ahead. I thought that cheaters were never supposed to win. What's the deal?

SINCERELY, UPSTANDING IN UPMINSTER

Dear Ups,

It is a sad truth that cheaters sometimes win. Just think of the long list of Hollywood spawn, hopped-up athletes, and crooked politicians (too boring to include here) who have made it big.

Perhaps you can find solace in the idea that these people are not truly happy. They haven't achieved success through merit and can therefore never truly take pride in their accomplishments. Of course, being bad people to begin with, this is probably not the case. They probably never reflect on their motives or methods long enough to feel remorse.

They're probably all sitting in some VIP lounge making out with celebrities and laughing at all the pathetic cog-in-a-wheel types, like you (and us) who try to get somewhere the hard way. Oh, well. Next question?

Dear DailyCandy,

I think you give really great advice. What did people do before you existed?

SINCERELY, SMITTEN IN SWINDON

Dear Smitten,

Hey, thanks. That's nice of you. You ask great questions. Please don't take anything we've said too seriously. We're not here to preach, but we do like to give new perspectives on life's dilemmas. Sometimes, we're even right.

Before DailyCandy, a time commonly referred to as BDC, there were many places for people to turn for advice that are still used throughout the world today. Horoscopes, runes, crystal balls, and palmistry have all been popular. Just about everyone's put two fingers on the Ouija board. The Magic 8-Ball has always been great. But while such methods will do in a pinch, your best guide is your own conscience. Unless, of course, you're a fascist dictator or criminally insane. Then the Magic 8-Ball is probably your best bet.

is for
RITUAL

 **rit • u • al** \ˈri-chə-wəl\ *n.* **1.** A religious ceremony. **2.** A habitual practice. **3.** That which justifies the purchase of designer yoga wear, tea paraphernalia, and other random items.

TO SOME, RITUAL MEANS SACRIFICING A VIRGIN

and two goats on the edge of an active volcano. To others, it's a bubble bath with Ella Fitzgerald playing in the background. Either way, ritual has played a big part in human survival and development.

On the surface, animal instinct and human ritual have a lot in common: Witness the cat who meticulously grooms herself and the schoolgirl who faithfully brushes her hair one hundred times before bed. The difference? As humans, we choose our rituals, and we can always decide to change or improve upon them. But no matter how many hair balls she coughs up, your cat will never wake up one day and say, "Why the hell am I licking myself? From now on, it's all showers for me."

So it's incumbent upon us as sentient beings to make sure our rituals remain meaningful and don't devolve into mindless habits. When rituals are good, they give us a sense of order and control, creating pockets of sanity amidst the chaos of our lives; when they're bad, they can lead to religious intolerance, narrow-mindedness, and unforgivable fashion choices. In this chapter we'll explore some of the ways you can incorporate ritual into your life.

*How to incorporate ritual into your
life in a healthy, helpful, and productive manner?
From taking a few extra moments in your day
to chill out to your favorite song to indulging in a crossword puzzle,
these are behaiviors the make life a little more manageable.*

YOU GOTTA
HAVE FAITH
Cool Rituals from World Religions

No journey into the realm of ritual would be complete without a pit-stop in that oh-so-popular cultural depot known as religion. Viewed as an unquestionable matter of faith by some, an outmoded adherence to obsolete ideals by others, religion is one of the most—if not the most—contested and conflict-inspiring subjects in history.

In other words, not necessarily prime DailyCandy territory. Still, having tackled such controversial subjects as lawyers-turned-jewelers, DIY bedazzled flip-flops, and the latest trends in fingernail art, we figured we weren't totally unqualified to tackle the subject. Below, then, is a list of some of our favorite rituals from religions around the globe, some brief history, and reasons why they're cool.

THE SABBATH (Judaism, Christianity, Islam)

ORIGIN: The creation story in these three monotheistic religions describes a week in which God made heaven and earth in what is generally agreed to be record time—six days—and rested on the seventh.

PRACTICE: People are commanded to rest on the seventh day of each week (Friday in Islam, Saturday in Judaism, Sunday in Christianity) and to honor it as a holy day, forgoing work and other "profane" activities.

WHY IT'S COOL: With the ever-blurring lines of private and public space, work and play time, we applaud anything that helps us carve out "sacred" time to chill out.

THE EUCHARIST (Christianity)

ORIGIN: At the Last Supper, Jesus instructs his disciples to eat the bread and drink the wine, explaining that the former is "his body" and the latter "his blood." The disciples, looking confused and a little freaked out, comply.

PRACTICE: Christians repeat this as a sacrament in church. For Catholics, the belief is not merely that bread and wine are symbols of Christ's body and blood, but are transubstantiated into it—they actually become it, and so the believer is ingesting a portion of the holy body.

WHY IT'S COOL: Sure, it's a little creepy. But then again, nothing brings home the idea of literally incorporating divinity into ourselves than this ritual.

KOAN PRACTICE (Zen Buddhism)

ORIGIN: The original meaning of the word is derived from the Chinese term for legal cases during the Tang dynasty.

PRACTICE: A zen koan is a parable or riddle which, from a strictly literal or logical perspective, is nonsensical or unanswerable. It is believed that through the contemplation of such a story and subsequent grasping of the essential nondualistic truth underlying all things, an individual can attain instantaneous enlightenment.

WHY IT'S COOL: Who doesn't wonder about the sound of one hand clapping?

HATHA YOGA (Hindu)

ORIGIN: A Hindu practice initiated by fifteenth-century Swami Swatamarama, hatha yoga is one of many forms of Hindu devotion.

PRACTICE: Yogis use physical postures and controlled breath to activate the various chakras or energy centers in pursuit of physical health and spiritual enlightenment.

WHY IT'S COOL: In addition to being one of the best forms of exercise and meditation ever, hatha yoga doesn't distinguish between spiritual and bodily health, instead seeing the two as integrated and correlated. In other words: cool.

HAJJ (Islam)

ORIGIN: The Koran commands Muslims to visit the holy city of Mecca at least once in their lifetime. It is considered one of the five pillars of Islam.

PRACTICE: The pilgrimage to Mecca, in order to "count," must take place during the Islamic month of Dhu al-Hijjah.

WHY IT'S COOL: In addition to bringing together people of common faith from throughout the world, the pilgrimage symbolizes the larger journey of life from a profane space and time toward a sacred one.

PEYOTISM (Native American)

ORIGIN: Use of peyote in pre-Columbian Americas began in the region now known as Mexico and spread to North America in the nineteenth century.

PRACTICE: Peyote, an edible cactus plant with hallucinogenic properties similar to those of acid, is taken in conjunction with meditation, prayer, and ritualistic dance; the "trip" lasts through the night and ends in the morning.

WHY IT'S COOL: Anyone who can build a lifestyle around a psyche-delic drug that doesn't involve tie-dyed shirts, dancing bears, repetitive music, and the phrase "I can totally *hear your hair, dude!*" is cool in our book.

UPGRADING YOUR HABITS TO RITUALS: A GUIDE

Sometimes everyday behavior just needs a simple tweak to turn it into a beautiful ritual. Here, a chart describing the difference.

NOT A RITUAL	RITUAL
BRUSHING YOUR TEETH	BRUSHING TEETH WHILE DANCING NAKED TO RAP MUSIC
SHOWERING	BATHING IN ASSES' MILK
EATING A TV DINNER	EATING YOUR FAVORITE TAKEOUT AND WATCHING *THE SIMPSONS*
NAPPING	NAPPING
PICKING AT YOUR FACE	GIVING YOURSELF A FACIAL
BITING YOUR NAILS	GETTING A MANICURE
SHOPPING	SHOPPING

Sometimes, just sometimes, what began as a life-affirming practice
becomes an exercise in useless drudgery or a nightmare of compulsive behavior.
Clearly not a good thing. Can you stop the madness? Of course you can.

CASE STUDIES:
OUT WITH THE OLD, IN WITH THE NEW
Updating Your Rituals

When it becomes necessary to give up a ritual, it's most important to replace it with something so as not to feel bereft. Here are a few examples of folks who've managed to quit bad habits by substituting new ones.

OUTMODED RITUAL #1
FELICIA'S FEATHERING

All through the late '70s, Felicia's grooming routine revolved around one central activity: feathering her frosted fringe into a Fawcett–Majors-esque barnet. Nothing started the day like that sacred ritual. But when her signature look fell out of favor in the early part of the next decade, Felicia was devastated. Then, one day, she caught sight of a fetching picture in a salon window: It was of a model sporting one of those newfangled asymmetrical 'dos. When the stylist informed her that with the purchase of something called a straightening iron she could achieve the look on her own, Felicia realized that not only had she found a new hairdo, she'd found a new morning ritual. And she lived happily ever after—or at least until the early '90s, when she had to start all over again.

RITUAL UPGRADE
Curling Iron to Flat Iron

BENEFITS
Stylish standards maintained; layers abandoned; hair-damage level, though not improved, kept constant; ritual reinstated.

CHOPPER'S COCKTAILS

Charles "Chopper" Chadwick was a good old boy. His ritual of choice, not surprisingly, was a prompt cocktail every evening at exactly 5:15 p.m., when he returned from work. Then one day his wife of twenty-five years, Valerie, informed him that if he didn't "lay off the sauce," she'd leave him. Chopper took the night to sleep on it and then decided it was probably best to give up the bottle— but only on the condition that Valerie would follow up his daily 5:15 p.m. glass of ginger ale with a round of raunchy sex. Valerie acquiesced, and they lived happily ever after.

RITUAL UPGRADE

Alcohol to Ginger Ale + Regular Sex

BENEFITS
Divorce averted; alcoholism overcome; sex had; ritual reinstated.

THEY SCREAMED FOR ICE CREAM

Heather, Trixie, Benita, and Ruthie had a Friday-night ritual involving horror movies and vast quantities of ice cream and other sweet treats. This worked great until they all hit the age of fifteen and were told by their doctors that they had officially joined that portion of the population that is morbidly obese. Trixie had an idea: Why not continue to get together, but rather than eat gallons of ice cream, eat healthy portions of frozen yogurt and watch foreign films? They all agreed to try it, and they lived happily ever after.

RITUAL UPGRADE

Ice Cream + Horror Movies to Frozen Yogurt + Foreign Films

BENEFITS
Weight loss; continued camaraderie; taste in films improved; arteries unclogged; ritual reinstated.

I have a stuffed monkey (with lifelike, soft rubber face, hands, and feet) named Bingo, and he sleeps in my bed. Whenever I make up the bed before leaving for a trip, I make sure Bingo is comfortable and lying on his back, so he'll be happy while I'm gone.

LENEER

My favorite rituals involve food that can only be found in certain countries/cities. When I arrive in New York, I go to my favorite hole-in-the-wall deli for an overstuffed hot pastrami sandwich. When I go to Venezuela, my family always has *arepas* (a type of corn bread patty) with *queso guayanes* (a type of cheese) ready for me. And as soon as I get back to England, I buy a bacon and egg sandwich from Marks & Spencer. (And I mean *as soon* as I get back; i.e., my friends take me straight from the airport, suitcases and all.)

MARY

I wake up to watch the sunrise on the last morning of any vacation.

ARI

I catch up on old newspapers and magazines when I fly. I read *Vogue* waiting to check in, polish off a *New Yorker* in the security line, and three fat *Vanity Fairs* on board. I deplane a whole carry-on lighter.

PETER

While I'm making coffee every morning I dip about ten Shreddies into Utterly Butterly margarine and eat them.

LISA

I clean the bathtub every day, just after I get out, with a facial cleansing wipe that I have used to take my makeup off!

KELLY

I think this is more OCD than a ritual, but when I set my alarm clock at night, I have to keep checking that the alarm is set until I get "the feeling" that it's set correctly. I flip back and forth from "wake up time" to "alarm set" anywhere from five to twenty times (but it could be more) until it feels like everything is set correctly and will work in the morning.

JERRY

I reread books compulsively. It started when I was seven and I read *Charlotte's Web* about fifty times, over and over again. Now I do it with all my favorite books, especially ones from childhood—*Chronicles of Narnia*, anything by Jane Austen.

ELLEN

HOPEFULLY YOU'VE LEARNED

a little bit about the value of maintaining certain practices—and the value of abandoning and improving others. One person's sacred ritual may be your idea of hell (see also: *hiking, camping, jury duty*) and vice versa, but part of having healthy routines is making sure we seek out new activities to partake in alongside the old, comfortable ones. And whether your favorite pastime is reading comic books or break dancing, bargain-hunting or making green jelly, always make time for it.

is for
SCORE

score \'skȯr\ *v.* **1.** To earn points in a sport or game *(He shoots, he* scores!*)* **2.** To achieve an advantage **3.** To get something for at least 30 percent off the retail price *(Oh, yes, this is a new Marc Jacobs coat. It was my* score *from the sample sale last week.)*

JOY COMES IN MANY FORMS.

Mozart symphonies, newborn pandas, make-you-weak-in-the-knees first kisses, walks on the beach, works of charity, curly fries. But nothing comes close to the sheer elation of finding a pair of Christian Louboutin boots for half off. Scoring a deal represents the perfect storm of human happiness: You get what you want, you get it for less, and you have the satisfaction of knowing you are smarter, more resourceful, and luckier than everyone else.

In pursuit of such rewards, we are willing to withstand a great many indignities. Long, desolate road trips to outlet malls. Teeming, angry crowds at sales and sample sales. Blisters. Fatigue. But all the gumption in the world won't get you far if you don't know some basic guidelines for finding your quarry. So read on, young shopper, and learn from the masters.

The game's just begun . . . and the early results are in.
Retailer: 0; You: 1.

CHEAP
VS. CHEAP
Telling the Difference Between
True Value and Total Crap

Sale!

Thrifty? Sure you are. Cheap? Well, that's a matter of opinion.
The point is, a bargain's not a bargain if what
you're ending up with is trash. A few ways to spot impostors:

LOOK AT THE SEAMS. If it's just a single line of stitches with a weak thread (i.e. if you can pull at the seam and pretty much look right through it), it's probably not very well made. Also, check to see that the seams line up properly: At a spot where four seams come together, they should all meet at the same point.

CHECK THE FABRIC CONTENT. One simple rule: Be concerned if it is highly flammable. Be on the lookout for acrylic, a man-made material that's often used in place of wool. While it has bulk and can feel soft, it doesn't have the same insulating properties and will not keep you as warm.

BEWARE OF IMITATION FABRICS with similar-sounding names or descriptions. Something made of "Cashmiracle" has never, you can bet your bippy, seen the underbelly of a goat. Something "silky" is almost definitely not made of silk. Jersey can be made from anything; satin is almost always synthetic. Pretty-sounding words like "ombre" and "taffeta" are no guarantee of quality.

TRY THE DARN THING ON. Often, poorly made items will only reveal their asymmetry and shoddiness on the body. Trying something on will alert you to itchiness (unlined wool pants, uncomfortable synthetics), scratchy seams and tags, and other sartorial offenses.

THE
TEN COMMANDMENTS
OF
SAMPLE-SALE ETIQUETTE

Little known fact: When Moses descended from
Mount Sinai, he was actually carrying three tablets. The first two
bore the familiar do-not-kill commandments.
The third, lesser-known one carried the ever important
guidelines to proper sample-sale behavior.

I
THOU SHALT NOT GO COMMANDO
UNLESS THERE ARE DRESSING ROOMS.

II
THOU SHALT WEAR A SKIRT IF THERE BE NO DRESSING ROOMS.

III
THOU SHALT NOT JUMP THE QUEUE.

IV
THOU SHALT NOT HIDE ITEMS.

V
THOU SHALT NOT ENGAGE IN THE FOLLOWING BEHAVIORS:
BITING, SCRATCHING, KICKING.
(Though shoving may occasionally be called for.)

VI
THOU SHALT ABIDE BY THE FIRST-COME, FIRST-SERVED RULE.

VII
THOU SHALT PAY BY CASH OR CREDIT CARD.

VIII
THOU SHALT BE POLITE TO THE SALES STAFF.

IX
THOU SHALT NOT PULL MADE-YOU-LOOKS
(as in, "Hey, is that Angelina Jolie?")
WHILE SWIPING SOMEONE'S SWEATER.

X
THOU SHALT COVET.
(Isn't that the point?)

HAGGLE ROCK

How Good Are Your Bargaining Skills?

Swap meets, flea markets, consignment shops,
foreign souks, and other informal shopping environ-
ments afford us the opportunity to wheedle,
bargain, and lowball. How sharp are your skills?

**1. THE OWNER OF YOUR LOCAL THRIFT STORE
SHOWS YOU A DRESS. THE FIRST WORDS OUT OF YOUR MOUTH ARE:**

a) "It's cute, but there's a stain on the back. Can I get it for half off?"

b) "It's a little out of my price range."

c) "Wow, only fifty pounds? What a steal!"

**2. YOU'RE IN THE MIDST OF A HEATED NEGOTIATION
WITH A RECORD-STORE SALESPERSON. YOU OFFER HIM £5 FOR A
BEAT-UP BECK LP. HE COUNTERS WITH £10. YOU:**

a) Walk away.

b) Say, "It's a deal!"

c) Offer him £7.

**3. A USED-CAR SALESMAN ASSURES YOU
HE'S QUOTING YOU THE BLUE BOOK PRICE. YOUR RESPONSE IS:**

a) "What's a Blue Book?"

b) "Hmmm. Show me a copy."

c) "Maybe so, but the model you're showing me
has been in two accidents and is missing a CD player,
which is supposed to come standard."

**4. THE BANGLE DUDE AT THE FLEA MARKET HAS
OFFERED YOU 10 PERCENT OFF IF YOU BUY THREE BANGLES.
YOUR RESPONSE IS:**

a) "Sold!"

b) "How about 15 percent?"

c) "Ten percent? That's only a quid fifty off.
I'll take three for the price of two."

5. WHEN TRYING TO MAKE A DEAL, YOU ALWAYS:

a) Offer about what you think it's worth.

b) Offer more than you think the item is worth. You wouldn't want to offend anyone.

c) Offer 25 percent less than you think it's worth.

ANSWER KEY:

1. a=3, b=2, c=1 2. a=3, b=1, c=2 3. a=1, b=2, c=3
4. a=1, b=2, c=3 5. a=2, b=1, c=3

SCORING:

11–15: THE NEGOTIATOR

You drive a hard bargain, oh fearless one. You'd go far as a used-car salesman, but think twice before burning bridges with salespeople you like at places you want to return to.

6–10: GOOD WILL HUNTING

You're a bit too inclined to play nice. You could step up your haggling chops a bit now and then, particularly when it comes to known overchargers like car dealers. The nice guy may not always finish last, but he rarely finishes first, either—and he usually goes broke trying.

1–5: I'M GONNA GIT YOU, SUCKA

Pathetic. You're probably more concerned with being liked than getting a deal, and as a result you have lots of friends and are constantly getting screwed by them. If you find that more often than not you're being taken for a ride, it's probably because you deserve it.

ARISTOTLE, quite the thrifty fellow himself, liked to say that everything we do stems from one or more of seven causes: chance, nature, compulsion, habit, reason, passion, and desire. So, when you think about it, getting a great deal is truly one of the most human pursuits imaginable, as it encompasses all seven elements. Some, however, might posit that the true value of a good deal attains a realm even higher than that.

Put another way: "To spend is human; to save, divine."

is for
TAKING A MOMENT

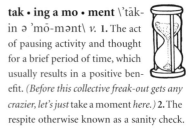

tak • ing a mo • ment \'tāk-in ə 'mō-mənt\ *v.* **1.** The act of pausing activity and thought for a brief period of time, which usually results in a positive benefit. *(Before this collective freak-out gets any crazier, let's just* take a moment *here.)* **2.** The respite otherwise known as a sanity check.

AMAZING, ISN'T IT,

how it takes takes only a split second to change your whole day. Chances are, you know what would make the biggest difference in your life. You just forget sometimes. Because, unfortunately, it's also true that sometimes it takes a long time to remember to take that moment to be nice to yourself (not to mention those around you).

So here's a list of handy reminders. Feel free to jot down your own ideas in the margins.

NAP.
USE THE CONFERENCE ROOM IF YOU HAVE TO.

BE NICE—JUST ONCE—TO A TELEMARKETER.
Think of how many times people scream at them every day. They're just trying to earn a living.

CRASH A PARTY.

WEAR A FLOWER IN YOUR HAIR.

MAKE UP
YOUR OWN
WORD.

MAKE SOUP.

INSTITUTE A DAILY CHOCOLATE BREAK.

WRITE A LETTER USING A COOL NEW PEN.

DONATE FIVE THINGS YOU DON'T NEED.

STOP WORRYING, YOU LOOK FINE.

WEAR A SLEEP MASK FOR THE HECK OF IT.

BREAK A LUNCH DATE; GET A MASSAGE INSTEAD.

BAKE COOKIES FOR A NEIGHBOR.

SEE A DOUBLE FEATURE.

SEND FLOWERS ANONYMOUSLY.

BORROW A FRIEND'S BABY FOR THE AFTERNOON.

MAKE PLANS.
BIG PLANS. LIKE, BORA BORA PLANS.

SAY NO, JUST FOR THE HELL OF IT.

LOOK UP A
WORD YOU DON'T KNOW.

SLEEP NAKED.

DON'T ANSWER YOUR MOBILE PHONE. *(You know you don't want to.)*

CALL A LONG-LOST CRUSH.

SET YOUR ALARM CLOCK
TO THE SALSA RADIO STATION.

REMEMBER,
YOU'RE NOT THE ONLY
ONE WITHOUT A
DATE ON SATURDAY NIGHT.

MAKE SNOW ANGELS.

VOLUNTEER
ON A SATURDAY
AFTERNOON.

MEET YOUR BEST
FRIEND FOR DRINKS AT 10 P.M.
ON A SUNDAY NIGHT.

STOP COUNTING CALORIES.

KEEP ONE ARTICLE OF CLOTHING FROM
SCHOOL AND WEAR IT EVERY FEW MONTHS.

INVITE YOUR PARENTS OVER FOR DINNER. COOK SOMETHING IMPRESSIVE.

PRETEND YOU'RE A MOODY FRENCH ACTRESS.

OVERTIP A CAB DRIVER

SEND YOUR FRIENDS
VALENTINES LIKE YOU USED TO
WHEN YOU WERE EIGHT.

TAKE A VACATION BY YOURSELF.
THE BEACH DOESN'T CARE IF YOU'RE SINGLE.

RESCUE AN ANIMAL.

SMILE,
EVEN WHEN YOU ARE TALKING
TO SOMEBODY
YOU DON'T LIKE.

CALL A FRIEND WHO YOU LOST TOUCH WITH.

TAKE A CLASS IN SOMETHING TOTALLY ESOTERIC, LIKE PALEOLITHIC MYTHOLOGY.

SING IN THE SHOWER, ELEVATOR,
OR ANYWHERE THAT HAS GOOD ACOUSTICS.

SEE A MATINEE—ALONE.

MAKE YOUR OWN WRAPPING PAPER.

HAVE AN EARLY-MORNING SNOWBALL FIGHT.

GO SKINNY-DIPPING AT MIDNIGHT
UNDER A FULL MOON.

• •

You get the picture, right? Before you know it, these moments of whimsy will become a habit. You'll have something to look forward to every day, and your day will look forward to what you bring to it.

is for
UPHEAVAL

up • heav • al \ˈəp-ˈhē-vəl\ *n.* **1.** A heaving up (duh). **2.** A sudden, violent change. **3.** Nasty circumstances that may require obscene portions of unhealthy food and/or psychotropic medication to endure. *(During a time of great* upheaval *last year, Arabella took to wandering the mall in her bathrobe, clutching a bag of beef jerky and self-help books.)*

LET'S NOT
MINCE WORDS, HERE.

Sometimes life sucks. Getting dissed, being laid off, losing loved ones, moving, dealing with unraveling friendships, and going up a pants size—upheaval is an inevitable part of life. As is the moment of truth when you have to hit the pillow and be alone with your anxiety.

And so, as we address the many aspects of everyday living, we felt it was important to explore its gloomier side as well.

Rock bottom? Not in your vocabulary.
For every crisis, there is a resolution. (Well, usually.)

FINDING SANITY LOANS:

These hypothetical scenarios outline common crises and potential resolutions. Feel free to add your own. Pregame strategy can be invaluable in getting to a successful outcome.

WHEN WORK'S NO FUN

CONFLICT: **Claudia has been working at the same company for six years. For the past year or so, she's been questioning whether she's following her true passion. Every morning she wakes up feeling stressed, depressed, and drained.**

RESOLUTIONS:

A) Claudia needs a new job.

B) Claudia needs to work with her boss to find new and more energizing work at her company.

C) Claudia might be depressed about something else she can't face, and is taking it out on work.

D) Claudia needs a shot of passion. Is there an unfulfilled hobby waiting in the wings? Night classes at the Cordon Bleu could do the trick.

OSCARINA THE GROUCH

CONFLICT: **Lisa is what you'd call bitter. Judgmental, accusatory, and combative. She gets annoyed with everything—especially her loving fiancé. She wonders if she should dump him.**

A) Someone is in a rut. She's possibly angry at her boss, her sister, her best friend. For whatever reason, she cannot address it with them, so she turns on her steady source of stability, her fiancé.

B) Lisa is engaged to the wrong man, but cannot face the truth because she's already engaged. She needs to be honest with herself.

C) Lisa needs to see a doctor about some happy pills. She could have a chemical imbalance that's making her anxious.

MIRROR, MIRROR ON THE WALL

CONFLICT: **Samantha has been complaining that she feels and looks ugly. She has bags under her eyes, and has developed a bit of a belly. Which isn't surprising considering she snacks all day, flakes out on her gym routine, and throws back six scotches a night.**

RESOLUTIONS:

A) Sammy needs to get back to the gym—fast. She needs to get moving; she needs to sweat. The endorphins will take over and do the rest.

B) Samantha is really hurt about something else in her life and is dealing with it by being self-destructive. She needs to address the source of the pain before she does more physical harm to herself.

C) Samantha's self-image may be out of whack. Maybe she was rejected by a suitor. Maybe she didn't get the modeling contract she was counting on. She needs to remember that beauty starts from within, and moves out from there. No one can look good if she doesn't feel good.

SLAVE TO LOVE

CONFLICT: **Tory has been seeing Max for two years. When she asks him where the relationship is going, he says he doesn't know. Max constantly makes Tory feel like she's not good enough. Like when she chooses a restaurant, he always complains that it sucks.**

RESOLUTION:

A) Tory needs to dump this bozo.

EMERGENCY CONTACTS
Preparing for Emotional Breakdowns

	SEMI-PYSCHO DESCRIPTION	EXAMPLE	WHO TO CALL
NEUROSIS	Anxiety, indecision, fear, obsession, phobias.	Nagging feeling that something bad will happen.	Confident, strong, patient, calming.
STRESS	Always rushed and nervous. Insomnia, adult acne.	Heart palpitations and looking haggard. A worry wart with a splotchy complexion to match.	Rational and pragmatic.
ANGER	Argumentative, aggressive, and belligerent.	You want to punch that woman because you hate her shoes.	Family is usually best. (They have to forgive your rudeness.)
VANITY	Beautiful, smart. (And did we mention beautiful?)	You're feeling damn sexy.	A crush or ex-lover.
HAPPINESS	Confidence, pride, and balance.	Everything feels smooth— even the kinks.	A hopeless romantic or optimist.
DESPERATION	Sad. Blue. No energy. Blah.	Too tired or bored to read this silly chart.	Warm and angelic.
EMBARRASSMENT	Insecurity to the nth degree.	Scared to go to a party or trendy restaurant alone.	Self-deprecator.
HYPER-ELATION	Ready to get this party started . . .	Antsy to get out and have some fun.	A jackass.
GUILT	Betrayed and manipulative.	Liar, liar, liar!	Noncerebral or religious type.
EGOTISTICAL/BITCHY	Feeling extra cool and ready to flaunt in-the-know prowess. Bravado.	I bought this and you can't have it . . . nyah, nyah.	Your mother.

Moods are like waistlines. They expand, range between high and low, and impact your outlook. Unlike changing waistlines, mood shifts are hard to predict and require crafty preemptive measures.

One of the best strategies for dealing with erratic mental states is to compile an emergency contact list of friends to call. Surely, you've noticed how certain people are better at calming your nerves, handling your bitchiness, and understanding your lunacy.

CONTACT NAME	E-MAIL/PHONE NUMBER

is for
VICE

vice \'vīs\ *n.* **1.** An evil action or habit **2.** A trivial fault or failing **3.** An activity that is at least ten times more fun while doing it than it seems the morning after. *(Strange how Sally's vice, those evil tequila body shots, seemed like such a good idea last night . . .)*

HISTORY SURE HAS BEEN CRUEL TO THE WELL-BEHAVED.

Nary an immortalization in song or verse. (Elvis was assuredly not referring to following instructions on a carton of OJ with "All Shook Up.") No imposing statues commemorating their accomplishments. ("The Man Who Always Politely Acquiesced Square" doesn't really roll off the tongue.) No songs called "Only the Good Die Old." Heck, nice guys very rarely appear in a feature film without being killed off halfway through.

The moral here? Bad behavior gets remembered. Whether you're an occasional jaywalker, a compulsive gambler, a serial shopper, or a notorious parole-breaker, your life probably owes some of its delightful unpredictability and thrill to vice. While we certainly don't advocate kidnapping babies, shoplifting, homewrecking, flashing strangers, or poisoning your boss, we do urge you to do something risky once in a while, and to celebrate being a little bit of a badass.

*An old man once said that ignorance is bliss. A totally hot indie
rocker in Austin once said that he was hung like a . . . oh wait, that's a different story.
Point is, in the world of vice it's best to know what you're dealing with.*

THE FACES OF SIN

Horizontal eating. Frequent glaring. Keeping the change. Normal
behavior, or telltale signs of vice lurking within one's very core? So
hard to tell; lesser mortals have spent their whole, sinful lives not
knowing. Never fear—this handy field guide identifies the key attributes of the classic vices.

VANITY

DRINK ORDER: "Coppola named this vintage after me, you know."
SHOE: Height-enhancing
FOOD: Minimal
WARDROBE: Ass-enhancing
FUEL: Compliments
ALIAS: Queen Drag, aka BacktoMe.org

ENVY

DRINK ORDER: "What's she having?"
SHOE: Roommate's
FOOD: A smaller steak than everybody else got, that's for sure.
WARDROBE: eBay'd movie set-castoffs
FUEL: Bad luck
ALIAS: Whiny McBratpants, aka The Biter

LUST

DRINK ORDER: "Whatever you're having, sailor."
SHOE: Matches lipstick
FOOD: Breakfast
WARDROBE: Minimal
FUEL: Orgasms
ALIAS: Titty von Sluttenson, aka Empress Handjob

DRINK ORDER: "Can you do the Guinness 'n' oyster cocktail with a Dom chaser?"

SHOE: Not those damn balance-confounding, drink-spilling heels

FOOD: Organ meat

WARDROBE: Expansive and expandable

FUEL: One more

ALIAS: Little Oinker, aka That Crusty Old Drunk

WRATH

DRINK ORDER: "Bring me a goddamn whiskey and bring it NOW."

SHOE: Shit-kickers

FOOD: Alka-Seltzer

WARDROBE: Chafing

FUEL: Can of whoop-ass

ALIAS: Bitchface

AVARICE

DRINK ORDER: "Tap water with four lemon slices, throw in a few spoons of sugar. Sheesh, fill it to the top!"

SHOE: As good as any of your frou-frou fancy ones

FOOD: Those pickled eggs on the bar are really filling.

WARDROBE: Reversible and convertible

FUEL: Double coupons

ALIAS: Stingy LaRue, aka Thrifty McCheapskate, Scion of El Cheapo

SLOTH

DRINK ORDER: "PBR me."

SHOE: Anything Velcro

FOOD: Chips. By the case.

WARDROBE: Suits. Of the sweat, track, and terry-cloth varieties.

FUEL: *Law & Order* reruns

ALIAS: Slugbert, aka Couchass

The life of the committed rule-breaker isn't all fun and games.
There are thrills to seek, lines to cross, and norms to flout—
not to mention walks of shame and nasty hangovers to survive.

ARE YOU GOING TO HELL?
Take our short quiz and find out!

Why feel guilty about eating too much and taking money out of your mum's purse if your afterlife is already guaranteed to be hot 'n' flamey? And if there's hope, better hang up your eatin' pants and shape up, cowgirl. We bet Virgil would have taken us up on the advance warning. Act now!

1. At a trade show in Birmingham, you're staring at the latest in toaster technology. As the waffle rises from its futuristic cradle, a stranger catches your eye. Turns out he's a sales rep from Ilford, but he definitely seems mysterious. When he proposes you join him and his colleague in a ménage à trois that night. You:

A) Pretend you thought he said, "*potage frambois*," and claim to be allergic to both soup and raspberries.

B) Agree to join them for dinner, but bail when they mention something about a saddle and wrestling masks.

C) Hand over your room keys and make a quick stop at the leather kiosk.

2. You're at a fab party. The spread is un-freaking-believable. Real classy. Like a commercial for financial planning. Toward the night's end, you notice a plastic bag in your purse. You:

A) Think "Doggie bag . . . doggie . . . MY DOG! That poor guy has been home alone and the Animal Planet show I leave on to keep him company (*K9 Karma* really seems to relax him) is long over. What kind of person am I?!" You thank your host and race home to McSnoodles.

B) Think "Doggie bag . . . doggie . . . HOT DOG! Now I know why that waiter looks familiar! He won that hot dog eating contest I entered but quit when I realized you had to eat the buns, too. Man, he was sexy." He passes with a tray of jalapeño poppers and you make eyes as you sensually devour one.

c) Think "DOGGIE BAG!!" And as you swill your scotch, shovel as much of the buffet as possible into your purse.

3. Your boyfriend calls from what sounds like a whorehouse. You've never actually heard a whorehouse, but you're pretty sure. He says he's "at the office" and won't make it to dinner. You:

A) Remind yourself that relationships are built on trust. And down a couple of extra Xanax so you're not a bitch when he crawls home.

B) Hang up and call his sister, and mention that he hasn't been eating or bathing and you think he might be addicted to crystal meth.

c) Tell him that's an amazing coincidence, because you're right by his office and were thinking of dropping by. Laugh as he squirms.

4. It's a weekday afternoon. You're in bed, enjoying some cake, when the phone rings. You let the machine get it. It's your neighbor. The glue gun she was using to make iPod cozies backfired and her finger is stuck to her cheek. She needs a ride to A&E. You:

A) Toss the cake aside and race to her house.

B) Pick up. Express sympathy, then explain you have a couple more hours of *The OC*, but if she can get to your house, you'll take her to A&E.

c) Listen as she blathers on, then throw the handset at the answering machine to stop the infernal racket. Turn over.

Scoring

MOSTLY A'S:
Harry Secombe has already told St. Peter all about you. You've got it made in the shade.

MOSTLY B'S:
Cut all the fun out of your life this very second. You've got a snowball's chance in hell of escaping eternal damnation.

MOSTLY C'S:
Do not pass go. You're going straight to hell.

HOW TO:
Turning Your Vice Into Virtue

Most often, fair miscreant, prissy squares are gonna be out to get you. They'll nag, they'll preach, they'll even criticize and call you nasty names. Remember: They're just jealous. Wagging of tongues and shaking of heads never killed anyone, and it's much easier to set naysayers straight than to get upset. Make them see the error of their ways with this useful list of retorts. Feel free to use verbatim:

THEY SAY YOU'RE VAIN.

YOU SAY: "Wow, sue me for actually washing my hair, putting on a face, and pressing my clothes, you nasty skank. Now shove off, you're blocking my sun."

THEY SAY YOU'RE ENVIOUS.

YOU SAY: "Hmph. I guess you think those reality stars actually deserve those lucrative mall-appearance fees. Where'd you get your shoes?"

THEY SAY YOU'RE GLUTTONOUS.

YOU SAY: "You know, more civilized people would call me a foodie. A bon vivant, if you will. *Bon Appetit* pays people to live like this, often slathered in foie gras. Have a sandwich, Skeletor."

THEY SAY YOU'RE LUSTY.

YOU SAY: "Just because I refuse to be shackled by society's antiquated and misogynistic notions of propriety doesn't mean my next orgy isn't going to be a kick-ass rager. Hey, do you guys swing?"

THEY SAY YOU'RE ANGRY.

YOU SAY: "How would you like it if your every waking moment pitted you against the world? You wouldn't like it one bit, wouldya, tough guy, WOULDYA?!" [Insert violent your-fist-their-head action here.]

THEY SAY YOU'RE GREEDY.

YOU SAY: "Go back to your Marxist rat hole, you commie pinko guerrilla! And paws off my Indigo Girls CD!"

THEY SAY YOU'RE SLOTHFUL.

YOU SAY: "Have another binger, and hey, while you're up, can you flex me the remote?"

AS YOU CAN SEE,

the world of vice is like playing the xylophone—dabbling a bit can be altogether pleasant, but too much and you're left with a splitting headache and angry looks from everyone around you. Finding balance is crucial, as pure innocence leaves a girl crippled by pent-up frustration and resentment, but total corruption is well, total corruption. So next time we're double-fisting it at a strip club, we'll look for you. Not on-stage, of course.

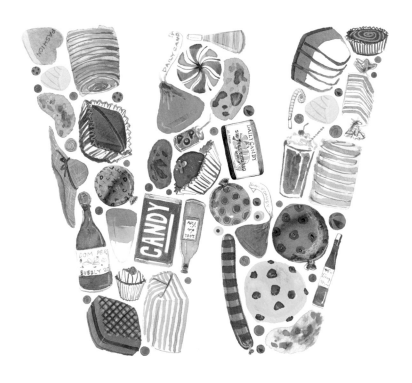

is for

WORK

work \ˈwərk\ *n*. **1.** Labor **2.** Employment; wage-earning **3.** A word whose meaning is lost on anyone with a job title beginning with the word "honorary" or ending with "emeritus." **4.** That which enables one to buy all sorts of unnecessary stuff *(I totally overspent at Liberty this weekend. But hey, I work really hard.)*

THOMAS EDISON ONCE SAID,

"Opportunity is missed by most people because it is dressed in dungarees and looks like work." Well, who can blame them? That doesn't sound like much fun, and most of us look pretty bad in dungarees.

Joking aside, work is the backbone of Western society. Without it, people couldn't earn money to buy fancy cars or vacations to Euro Disney. Work is what gives us a sense of accomplishment, allows us to contribute something to the world, and provides us with the opportunity to use phrases like "hump day" and "TGIF." (Not to mention the impermeable excuse, *"Gotta run! Got work to do!"*)

This chapter is devoted to examining the various ways in which what we do affects our lives—and how we can be better, more successful, and less accident-prone workers. (Okay, not that last thing.) Because what we choose to do for a living can say a lot about us, or a little—but either way, most of us will spend a full third of our adult lives in the workplace. So whether you're just temping or pursuing your ultimate dream (or both), who you are at work is a large part of who you are. Remember that the next time you're eavesdropping on the personal conversations of the chick in the next cubicle or writing nasty things about your boss on the bathroom wall.

*There as many different jobs out there as there are people.
How to find your calling? Mull your options, examine your choices,
and see where others have been.*

ODD JOBS

*DailyCandy Staffers
Reveal Their Weirdest
Work Experiences*

What did you think—that we were all born into our fabulous jobs? Ha.
Here's just a sampling of the odd jobs previously held by DailyCandy
employees before they found their present employment:

I was a cashier for three weeks at a Cambodian gay burger joint
called Hot 'n' Hunky. My boss would smoke under the
CAM HUOK THOC sign, which means "no smoking."

C.M.

I worked in a neuropsychiatric lab where we did mini brain surgeries
on rats. Then we cut off their heads with a mini guillotine and sliced up their
brains on a machine that looked like a mini deli slicer.

E.E.

I worked as an intern at an aquarium, thinking I would be able to
swim with the dolphins. Instead, my duties included recording and observing
how many times a day the sea otters would masturbate. They masturbated a lot.

A.T.

The summer Viagra was launched, I worked for their PR agency.
It was my job to monitor the international press for mentions of erectile
dysfunction. So there I would sit, alone, day in, day out, scouring
papers from around the world and clipping out anything to do with penises.

D.R.

I worked at Spencer Gifts. You know, the store that
pretends to sell gifts but is really a store for dirty old men to get a porn
fix while shopping with their families?

C.F.

At fifteen, I worked as a hostess in a deranged restaurant
that turned into a nightclub on the weekends. But really,
I was the lookout for chefs who screwed various waitresses (looking to
get better shifts) in the shed where we kept the nonperishables.

J.G.

I was the waitress screwing the chefs.

B.S.

ENEMIES

We've all had one: that perky whippersnapper whose mission in life
is to steal your thunder and make you look bad. How to
know when to disarm, when to fight back, and when to destroy?
Below, a comeback for every undermining statement.

SHE SAYS	YOU SAY
"GOOD IDEA— I HAD THE SAME ONE LAST WEEK!"	"GREAT MINDS THINK ALIKE."
"I LOVE YOUR BLOUSE. DID YOU GET IT AT PRIMARK?"	"NO, BUT LEAVE IT TO YOU TO KNOW WHERE TO FIND THE BEST ARMANI KNOCKOFFS."
"ARE YOU OKAY? YOU LOOK TIRED."	"AH, WELL. BURNING THE MIDNIGHT OIL WILL DO THAT TO YOU."
"I CAN'T WAIT UNTIL I'M IMPORTANT ENOUGH TO TAKE THREE-HOUR LUNCHES."	"ME NEITHER! THEN WE CAN GO TOGETHER."
"I HEARD HOW YOU GOT FIRED FROM YOUR LAST JOB. HOW AWFUL FOR YOU."	"AND I HEARD HOW YOU ALWAYS GO DIGGING FOR DIRT ON YOUR COWORKERS. HOW DESPERATE OF YOU."
"AREN'T YOU AFRAID THAT YOUR AGGRESSIVENESS WILL COME OFF AS MASCULINE?"	"FUNNY—I WAS GOING TO ASK YOU THE SAME THING ABOUT YOUR MUSTACHE."
"I READ SOMEWHERE THAT OVERWEIGHT PEOPLE ARE LESS LIKELY TO BE PROMOTED. DOES THAT BOTHER YOU?"	"NOT AS MUCH AS THE STATISTICS ON UGLY PEOPLE MUST BOTHER YOU."
"HOW DO YOU GET IT ALL DONE? I GUESS IT HELPS TO BE SINGLE."	"ACTUALLY, NO, THAT'S NOT MUCH HELP. BUT BEING REALLY WELL EDUCATED HAS BEEN AWESOME."
"YOU REMIND ME A LOT OF MY MOM."	"THAT'S FUNNY, BECAUSE YOU REMIND ME A LOT OF MY TWO-YEAR-OLD."
"WOW, I BET I REMIND YOU OF A YOUNG YOU!"	NOTHING. THEN DESTROY HER.

THE DOS & DON'TS OF WORKING AT HOME

Some of the things you don't have to do when you work at home: bathe, brush your teeth, wear a suit, wear anything at all, miss daytime telly, see people, apply concealer, scrounge for bus fare, get out of bed, ever stop eating.

Sound like a dream? Yes and no. Working at home is a complicated exercise in discipline and sloth that only a rare few have perfected. Here's how they do it:

DO

GET OUT OF BED. Even if you have a laptop. Even if it's to drag your ass to the next room.

GET DRESSED. Oh, not every day. But once in a while, just to remind yourself what it feels like—and to throw those jammies in the laundry.

MAKE APPOINTMENTS OUTSIDE THE HOUSE. The occasional lunch or drinks meeting gets you out into the world.

HAVE SET WORK HOURS. This one's tough. It's easy to let your work day bleed into your personal time when it all happens in the same place. Stick to a schedule and put away your work when the day is done.

HAVE A SEPARATE WORK SPACE. And no, we don't mean the other side of the bed. Even if it's just a special corner of your studio flat, make sure you have a dedicated area.

LET FRIENDS KNOW THAT EVEN THOUGH YOU'RE AT HOME, YOU'RE AT WORK. It's easy to get caught up in nonwork activities when you work at home—particularly talking on the phone. Limit personal phone conversations the same way you would at an office for maximum productivity.

ADOPT A PET. You're the perfect owner.

LOVE WHAT YOU DO. It's the only way. Even the most disciplined person in the world will find ways to skive off work at home unless he or she really enjoys doing it.

DON'T

EAT EVERYTHING IN THE FRIDGE. This is very tempting, as no one is watching you and the fridge is right there. Set regular meal hours, just as you would if you were a normal person.

ISOLATE. IT'S ALL TOO EASY TO FEEL LONELY. If you have colleagues who also work at home, make sure to meet once in a while for coffee or a working day together.

BECOME ADDICTED TO ONLINE SHOPPING. This can happen. All too easily. One minute you're surfing idly for a designer bag. The next you're obsessively checking eBay to see if they have any vintage Vivienne Westwood shoes. For example.

WATCH SOAP OPERAS. That's depressing. If you must, TiVo or tape them and watch them after the work day is over.

EVER, EVER COMPLAIN. If you can make it work, you have a dream job.

MOST AGREE that there are plenty of pursuits more exciting, intriguing, and stimulating than the labor they're paid to do. But, if you're lucky, getting up every day and showing up at your job is inching you ever closer to that larger goal of being your own boss, being the boss of a lot of other people, or simply doing what you love for a salary you can live on.

Plus, the urge to blow off work has been known to lead to major problems like unemployment, loss of self-esteem, or the penning such tired euphemisms as "man of leisure" and "in between opportunities." And if the threat of ending up there doesn't get you out the door, nothing will.

is for
X

x \'eks\ *n.* **1.** The twenty-fourth letter of the alphabet. **2.** The Roman number ten. **3.** An indeterminate amount or quantity. **4.** An illegal substance popularized by the advent of rave culture. **5.** A symbol for the elimination of something or someone undesirable or detrimental.

FACE IT: Whether good (the ten-day Caribbean beach vacation complete with a fling with the cabana boy), bad (the blind date who talked on his mobile phone throughout dinner), or otherwise, all things come to an end. Endings are as natural a part of life as beginnings.

Sad? You bet. Manageable? But of course. (Hey, this is *DailyCandy A to Z*, not a Samuel Beckett play.) Any which way you slice it, goodbye, *adios*, or *arrivederci* is often hard—but in embracing life's endings, we embrace an essential part of the human experience. So, as the alphabet winds its way to completion, and we find ourselves rounding the corner on Y and Z, we thought we'd send you off with some helpful hints on how to make the best of letting go.

Parting with people is hard. Parting with your stuff?
Impossible—for some people, anyway. A few pointers from
an expert on how to clear away the cobwebs.

THROWING
THINGS AWAY
A Soon-to-Be-Non-Owner's Guide

Why do most of us hold onto things we don't need? Sentimental value? An irrational belief that someday, for some reason, we will eventually need them? Yes, and yes. But it's more than that—it's a sort of inability, when faced with mountains of stuff, to really know what has value and what doesn't.

The solution: Learn to trust your opinion. Ask the following three questions about every item in your possession to give yourself permission to throw things away.

1. WHEN'S THE LAST TIME I USED THIS? This applies to clothing, exercise machines, kitchen gadgets, pieces of paper, rocking chairs, hair-care products—pretty much anything. If the answer is a year ago or more, it's time to get rid of it.

2. DO I HAVE MORE THAN ONE OF THESE? The truth is, no one really needs more than one bullhorn. No one needs more than one washing machine. And no one needs twelve pairs of Converse One Stars. Okay, maybe some of us do. But the point is, if you've got lots of duplicates, you might consider parting with the extra items.

3. DOES THIS HAVE GENUINE SENTIMENTAL VALUE? If you haven't used it in a while there's only one other reason to hold on to it: It has meaning beyond its basic function. But it could be that you're a little promiscuous with the sentimental value: Is it really possible to feel an attachment to the necklace Brad Dunn gave you in sixth form when you can't even picture what Brad Dunn looks like anymore? Does that Disneyland souvenir really take you back to happier times? (Wasn't that you who threw up on your sister right after riding Space Mountain?)

There's no other way to put it: Some people just suck.
They're users, jerks, liars, or just plain dumb. When it comes to such useless types,
there's only one thing to do: Push the eject button. In the ebb and
flow of life, nasty fallings-out happen. Best to approach them prepared.

THIS IS THE END, MY FRIEND
Platonic Breaking Up Is Hard to Do

These are sticky situations. All the usual excuses won't cut it. So how to know when it's time to extricate yourself from an unwanted or unhealthy relationship? We figured men are the experts in this department, so we stole a page from their playbook. So here it is: the stages of friendship in decline, presented as a series of sports metaphors.

STAGE ONE
The Starting Lineup

This is normally where she starts. A part of the GNO (Girls' Night Out). A card-carrying member of the Sunday-night DVD club. A favorite on speed dial. But remember, the starting lineup is reserved for the best players on your team. Your reliable last-minute movie date. Your 2 a.m. just-got-home-from-a-hot-date phone call. Your you-sound-sad-come-over pal. Spaces on this list should not be given out to someone who doesn't return your calls, flirts with your guy, or talks trash about you. If she's failing your expectations, take her out of the rotation.

STAGE TWO
Bench Her

So, she's been benched. This should give her plenty of time to reflect on her behavior, all in the hopes, of course, that she'll recognize that she hasn't been giving her best. A key point to any benching, however, is to make sure she is aware that the game goes on without her. How? Cc her on e-mails recapping last weekend's debauchery. Forward her your pics from the weekend at the lake house. Text message her from drinks with friends, but don't invite her to join. Evil? Yes, maybe. But if she truly wants back in the game, odds are she'll step up to the plate.

STAGE THREE

The Minor Leagues

No attitude adjustment for your player means a major demotion to the AAA farm team. And yes, this is as out-in-the-boonies as it sounds. The only reasons to call her back up to the premiership at this point are purely selfish. She's invited to a party that you want to go to. She's friends with a guy you want to meet. Or if you're in need of a last-minute wingman and the rest of your list is out for the night. This stage is all about what she can do for you. Give and take struck out a long time ago.

STAGE FOUR

Career-Ending Injury

The CEI can come at any point in your player's career, even averaging 50 in your starting lineup. (Confused? It's okay. Just go with it.) Examples of CEIs include: hooking up with your crush (preposterous!), telling your secrets to other friends, blowing you out multiple times, not being there for you during a breakup or a layoff, and telling a boldface lie ("I did not ruin your dress—it came with that stain on it"). All of which send her directly into early retirement.

STAGE FIVE

Early Retirement

Now it's time to officially say good-bye. Odds are, however, she's already alienated you to such a degree that no formal conversation is necessary. You may thus avoid the "It's not you, it's me" at your neighborhood Starbucks. Go ahead; delete her name from your mobile phone. Take her e-mail address out of your contact list. She is now a free agent, and you no longer owe her a thing.

POST-BREAKUP REACTIONS
What Not To Do

Every girl is allowed a post-breakup psycho grace period. But when your 48 hours are up, no more boiling bunnies or sobbing to his best friend. Make a clean break and try your darnedest to do the following:

LIMIT GOOGLING HIM TO THE FIRST 24 HOURS.
Rereading his marathon time over and over again will only depress you.

DO NOT, UNDER ANY CIRCUMSTANCES, CALL HIS MOTHER.
Or anyone related to him.

DO NOT CALL AND HANG UP.

DO NOT TEAR UP ALL OF YOUR PICTURES OF HIM.
One day you will want to remind yourself of just how hot he was. Trust us.

DO NOT STOP EATING.
Although you'll be skinny for the next five minutes, odds are as soon as you get out of your funk you'll pack the pounds back on—and then some.

NO DRIVE-BYS.
You're right, he will see you. No, that's not a good thing.

DO NOT TEXT MESSAGE HIM JUST TO SEE HOW HE IS.
What will knowing that he's doing just fine do for you?

STOP SLEEPING IN HIS OLD T-SHIRT.
It isn't cute. It's pathetic.

DO NOT E-MAIL HIM A PROCLAMATION OF YOUR LOVE,
a diatribe of how he wronged you, or a settlement agreement (as in who gets the dog, the friends, the coffeemaker). Leaving a paper trail of your insanity is never a good idea.

You Do the Maths:

WHEN IT'S OKAY TO DATE A FRIEND'S EX

It's a simple equation. Length of relationship (in months) divided by degree of separation plus one month (just for good measure) equals wait time (period in months).

ASSIGNING DEGREES OF SEPARATION VALUES:

FRIEND = 1

FRIEND OF A FRIEND = 2

FRIEND OF A FRIEND OF A FRIEND = 3

(AND SO ON UNTIL YOU REACH KEVIN BACON)

Let's try it together.

Your friend breaks up with Tony after going out with him for a year.	12 divided by 1, + 1 = 13	You must wait a year and one month.
Your friend's friend breaks up with Andrew after dating for a year.	12 divided by 2, + 1 = 7	You must wait seven months.
Your friend's friend's friend breaks up with Marcus after dating for a year.	12 divided by 3, + 1 = 5	You must wait five months.
Your best friend breaks up with Jonathan after dating for .1 months.		NEVER. (Trick question.)

SO WHAT HAVE WE LEARNED? Well, letting go is an important part of living. And while it can be painful, it's often the occasion for bringing new and wonderful things into our lives. So as one door closes, another opens. Though this chapter comes to its inevitable end, as surely as spring follows winter, another follows it. And another after that. And another—oh, well, actually, there are only two chapters left, so that really will be the end. Sorry.

is for

YIKES

yikes \'yīks\ *interj.* **1.** A word used to express a strong reaction, such as embarrassment or surprise. *(Yikes! I cannot believe I walked out of the ladies' room with my skirt tucked into my panties!)*

SOME PEOPLE DON'T GET EMBARRASSED.

They're either so unself-aware that they don't notice when they've said or done something horrifying, or they're perfectly self-aware and just don't care.

Thankfully, we don't know many of those people. Here at DailyCandy, we believe life is really just a series of humiliations strung together by the occasional uneventful meal or restless night's sleep. And though the price we've paid for such a lifestyle is high—social anxiety, dashed dreams, crushed egos—it's all been worth it, because it means we could bring you this chapter. So we present Yikes: our most embarrassing moments,* provided for your reading pleasure.

* Names have been omitted to protect the mortified.

I ONCE HAD TO WALK into an investor meeting covered head-to-toe in cement after having been covered with the stuff by a malfunctioning cement mixer.

Unfortunately, while my plan had been to pop my head in, explain what had happened, and excuse myself, by the time I got through the first sentence the cement had hardened sufficiently that I couldn't move and had to be carried out.

• •

WHEN I WAS IN FIFTH GRADE, my mum took me to see one of the stars of *Eastenders* at some downtown festival. She put me in the queue with all these old women and sat by the sidelines as I inched forward.

So I got up to the front, and the actress pulled out a photo and said something I couldn't quite make out. So, assuming she asked me what I wanted her to write, I answered, "Oh, I don't care."

She looks at me and screams, "WHAT? You don't care that my name is TA-KAY-SHA (or something like that)?!" And I'm scared to death, so I say nothing. She screams that she's not signing any more autographs today for ungrateful fans like me. Then she leaves. And everyone, and I mean everyone, freaks out and starts yelling at me.

• •

MY VERY FIRST INTERVIEW was to be a clerk at the *Times*. I was nervous as all get-out. So I woke up, got myself dressed in my most conservative outfit, and started walking to the interview, trying to muster a confident stride. It was a really windy day, and things were blowing all over. Newspapers and rubbish from the pavement blew up into my hair, and one finally hit me smack in the face. I brushed it off, and tried to regain my composure—only to realize that something smelled terrible. Really terrible. Rancid beyond words. I wiped my brow and looked down at my hand.

Two words: dog shit. All over my face. So much for pooper-scooper laws . . .

• •

I WAS STAYING AT A HOTEL in L.A. where I was getting a really good deal on the rate because it was under renovation. I'd been traveling a lot, and my sleep schedule was a bit wonky (to say the least), which manifested itself in my waking up in the middle of the night not knowing where I was. This progressed into a sleepwalking habit where I would wake up and start opening closet doors, frantically looking for something. (What on earth for I have no idea—save that for the shrink.)

One particular night—and here's where I have to admit that I sleep naked—I was awakened by the slam of a door. I looked around and realized I had walked out of my hotel room and locked myself out. I looked everywhere for a linen closet, a sheet or a towel . . . anything . . . but no cigar. So I did the only thing I could do: I went downstairs and peered around the corner to the front desk, where a large heavyset man was reading the paper. He sweetly gave me his jacket and took me back up to my room to let me in.

I went back to sleep, and the next day went out to get him a bottle of champagne before I checked out—to say thank you. The receptionist informed me that he never showed up for work the next day. Never called, just flew the coop.

• •

AT A HUGE FAMILY DINNER with a boyfriend at a fancy resort, his father kept bringing me drinks during cocktail hour. As we finally sat down and they were bringing the salad, they placed mine in front of me and I passed out in the salad plate. Boyfriend carried me ("Like," his mother said, "the baby she is") back to the room with salad all over my face. We broke up soon after.

• •

ON A TV SHOOT for a big department store, I reconnected with the store's head of PR, with whom I'd been professionally friendly for years but whom I hadn't seen in at least a year. Since our last encounter, a lot had happened. She'd gotten married and changed her name, bought a flat, etc. As we caught up, it struck me that her belly was rounded, as if with child. Wow, how exciting, I thought. I wanted to be the sort of friend who noticed these precious moments, and I wanted to congratulate her. Against all conventional wisdom and common sense, I put my hand on her tum-tum and cooed, "And is there a baby in there????"

"No, there isn't," she snapped.

ONE EVENING I WENT OUT TO DINNER with my boyfriend. Walking home, my boyfriend decided to call his friend Mike, to see if we could stop by. His friend said to come on over. As we continued to walk, I felt a little cramp in my stomach. We called up to the little flat on the third floor. As we started to walk up the stairs, the cramps progressed. It was apparent then that I had to use the bathroom. So we walk into the small, hot flat and I couldn't even say hello to Mike or his flatmate—just "Where's the bathroom?"

I ran to the small, windowless bathroom. Well, you know what happened next. I was sitting there, realizing that there was not one other sound in the flat. Nothing. Just me and the music of my bodily functions.

I was dying from the heat, so I began to take off my clothes. When it got really bad, I did what any girl in my situation would do: I flushed (create some noise, make it seem like it wasn't taking as long, you know the drill). As the water level began to rise rapidly, my body again started acting up. I didn't know what to do so I politely called my boyfriend's name. He came to the bathroom door. He almost fainted when he opened it, but I told him that he needed to get a plunger. So he asked Mike for a plunger. When he came back with the plunger, he told me to get off the toilet—and I couldn't. So here we were, I was half naked in a hot smelly bathroom with my boyfriend watching, yelling at me to move. When it finally ceased, I had to get into the shower and watch him plunge while my you-know-what was splashing all over him, all over the walls, gagging. It was horrifying, but of course I was laughing. He was yelling.When it was all over, he threw the plunger at me in the shower, where I had to wash it, me, and the bathroom walls. Once clean, I tried to regain my composure, got dressed, and exited the bathroom, only to find the three boys sitting there in silence. I said, "Excuse me, I have to go," and ran out the door and all the way home.

WELL, THERE YOU HAVE IT.

We showed you ours; now go forth and share your stories of horror and humiliation with the world. Yes, you'll relive the embarrassment. Yes, you'll have to admit you're not perfect. And yes, others will laugh and point. But if this chapter has taught you anything, it's that they do that anyway.

is for

ZEITGEIST

zeit • geist \'tsīt-gīst\ *n.* **1.** The thought and spirit of a period of history; a shared worldview **2.** That which marketing firms, ad executives, and consumers are driven to pursue with blind, rapacious fervor. **3.** A term whose meaning no one really seems to understand but which everyone throws around with reckless abandon.

USED TO BE, THE TERM "ZEITGEIST"

was blithely applied to entire centuries and hemispheres. Then, it was perfectly acceptable to use it to refer to the collective character of a generation. Nowadays, however, the world moves faster—and, consequently, a particular "spirit of the age" can really only be said to last as long as the rotation period of its most quotable beer commercial (see also: The Great "Wazzaaaaaaaa!" Era). Like our cars, our computers, and our media, zeitgeist is an elusive, ever-evolving beast, and take it from us—it's a bitch to keep track of.

It is, after all, DailyCandy's job to bring you a bite-size bit of zeitgeist every day.

In this book, however, we've put aside our usual task of tracking the latest, greatest, newest thing for the purpose of bringing you our thoughts on less fleeting matters: family, friends, work, and other fundamentals of life. (Oh, and yes, some stuff on dealing with skanky men and fad diets.) And in doing so, we've realized something: The basic rules for success and happiness in both realms are really the same: Trust your instincts. Be confident. Be humble. Stay curious. Exchange ideas. Laugh at yourself. Laugh at others. And for heaven's sake, don't wear stuff that looks bad on you.

While in the course of doing our jobs, we've occasionally played the role of breathless trend-of-the-minute pushers, what more often guides our choices are the standards above. Both in this book and in our daily e-mails, we've tried to write about what we think is worth talking about, and to do it in a voice that's authentically our own. So the best advice we can offer on being up on the zeitgeist is this: You already are. Don't try to nail it down. Be guided by your own ideas, opinions, and tastes. That way you'll end up steering the spirit of the age, which is way better than trying to play catch-up with it. And never, ever, take it too seriously. As the great German thinker August Everding said, "Whoever marries the zeitgeist will be a widower soon." (Okay, fine. We don't really know who that guy is, but he sounds pretty smart.)

But who are we kidding? You know this stuff already. In the intro to this book we claimed that DailyCandy is a state of mind, a way of looking at the world. So the "wisdom" offered in these pages is really just DailyCandy's own mini-zeitgeist, you might say. And as such it is also the indirect product of our relationships with you, our readers, who never fail to tell us when we've made you laugh, made you think, or made you really, really irritated. Our success, continuance, and very existence are due to your ongoing interest and input. So we guess all we really want to say here is this: Keep on doing what you're doing. And we will too.

Oh, and we hope you liked the book.

See you tomorrow.

Before We Go, a Few Thank-Yous

This book has been touched by many hands, but truly molded by a few. Through the late nights, volumes of copy, and floods of e-mail, three women poured their hearts and souls into these pages. Without Dany Levy, Pavia Rosati, and Eve Epstein, there would be no book.

Thank you also to DailyCandy's other kick-ass editors: Sonya Castex, Jeralyn Gerba, Lindsey Kanter Gladstone, Alexandra Hall, Ashley McAdams, Crystal Meers, and Dannielle Romano all gave their brilliant words, insight, humor, and time, as did writers Michele Wissot, Leonora Epstein, and Deanna Kizis. Moreover, we wish to convey our gratitude to the entire DailyCandy staff for sharing their stories, memories and, most important, their horrifically embarrassing moments.

A special thank-you to Sujean Rim for her stunning illustrations; most every compliment we receive about DailyCandy includes a comment on her charming artwork. And we wouldn't have gotten far without the motivating words (read: bitch-slaps) of DailyCandy CEO Pete Sheinbaum.

Of course, this book would never have existed without an agent to sell it—or, in this case, two: Our special thanks to Suzanne Gluck and Andy McNicol at the William Morris Agency for their encouragement and support. Huge props to Number Seventeen (Bonnie Siegler, Emily Oberman, and Allison Henry) for their impeccable, spot-on design—we couldn't have wished for a more beautiful book. And finally, everyone knows the secret brains behind any book are its editors. So a big thanks to Kelly Notaras and the entire team at Hyperion.